GARY GOODRIDGE

AND

MARK DORSEY

ECW Press

Published by ECW Press
2120 Queen Street East, Suite 200, Toronto, Ontario, Canada M4E 1E2
416-694-3348 / info@ecwpress.com

LIBRARY AND ARCHIVES CANADA CATALOGUING IN PUBLICATION

Goodridge, Gary
Gatekeeper : the fighting life of Gary "Big Daddy" Goodridge
/ Gary Goodridge and Mark Dorsey.

ISBN 978-1-55022-993-6
ALSO ISSUED AS: 978-1-77090-071-4 (PDF); 978-1-77090-070-7 (EPUB)

1. Goodridge, Gary. 2. Martial artists—Canada—Biography.
1. Dorsey, Mark II. Title.

GV1113.G66A3 2012   796.8092   C2011-902849-2

Editor for the press: Michael Holmes
Cover design: Marijke Friesen
Cover photo: Peter Lockley
Interior photo images courtesy of Gary Goodridge
Printing: Webcom   1   2   3   4   5

For the publication of *Gatekeeper* we acknowledge the financial support of the Government of
Canada through the Canada Book Fund for our publishing activities, and the contribution of the
Government of Ontario through the Ontario Book Publishing Tax Credit. The marketing of this
book was made possible with the support of the Ontario Media Development Corporation.

PRINTED AND BOUND IN CANADA

For Quenell, Trinity and Tyra,
my (chicklets) three beautiful daughters

PREFACE

A lot of mixed martial arts autobiographies have hit shelves in the past few years. Their collective success is inextricably linked to their subjects: Randy Couture, Chuck Liddell, Tito Ortiz, Matt Hughes, B.J. Penn, and so on. On top of the fact that their names alone would help sell books, these fighters, their fights, and their stories are so tightly woven into the fabric of MMA that it seems necessary to read their memoirs.

Chronicling Gary Goodridge's journey is crucial for an altogether different reason.

Because MMA is rooted in the undying question of who is the "best fighter," its finicky onlookers tend to fetishize and dismiss anything less than absolute dominance. In this respect, MMA might be the ultimate "What have you done for me lately?" sport. Gary "Big Daddy" Goodridge was one of those fighters who helped to counteract this indifference: no one ever believed he would win a UFC tournament, a Pride heavyweight title, or the K-1 World Grand Prix, and yet his presence — which brought with it a promise of violence — became something that deeply excited fans. Big Daddy was one of the first fighters to make being a hard-swinging gatekeeper both valuable and engrossing.

Better still, he was suited to the role: Goodridge was a take-no-prisoners brawler who openly admits his indifference to — perhaps even contempt for — everything that isn't haymakers and headsmashing. Many like to believe that MMA preserves some ancient gladiatorial ethos about the valor and courage it takes to fight, and the idea of fighting anyone, at any time. Part of what makes Goodridge so intriguing is how he embodies that ethic while cutting through the bullshit: from the moment he debuted as a dubious "Kuk Sool Won" specialist and hacksawed into Paul Herrera's head with his elbow, Goodridge has stood in opposition to the mysticism of martial arts.

Few MMA competitors have the depth and breadth of stories that Goodridge has. He is a unique thread in the tapestry of the sport. The first 13 seconds of his bout against Herrera became some of the most famous — and *infamous* — in MMA history. For 15 years he fought the who's who of MMA and K-1. He played opponent to Coleman and Frye, then later Nogueira and Emelianenko. His August 2002 upset of K-1 stalwart Mike Bernardo was a crucial moment in changing the collective opinions about the nature of striking and the caliber of athletes in both MMA and K-1. Goodridge was an unapologetic brawler: few fighters have ever committed themselves or more honestly subscribed to the notion of fighting any man, anytime, anywhere.

Tragically, it is that same mentality that has made him one of the starkest and most chilling examples of what a reckless career in prizefighting can do to a competitor.

Fans of MMA and kickboxing like to believe that for a host of reasons, from rule structures to bout length, their sports are safer than boxing, where retired athletes often degenerate into frail, dementia-addled husks of their former selves, or football, where repeated concussions show their devastating impact long after players leave the gridiron. And yet, here is Gary Goodridge, once a fearsome physical specimen who was both charming and articulate, reduced to a punching bag.

What makes his writing so refreshing is its honesty. Goodridge is keenly aware of how lamentable and even pathetic his predicament is. He admits he can barely train, and that given his physical state, such effort might not even be worth it. He knows he should hang them up and not be the "organic punching bag" — his words — that he's become. And yet, he fights on, not having tasted victory in years, chasing paydays. Most assume that a fighter's refusal to hang them up is born of delusion and the hope he can once again reach the heights he once enjoyed. Goodridge's words aren't deluded, and they convey the legitimate sickness and longing that is often behind a fighter's inability to lay down his sword.

Part of what made Goodridge so magnetic for fans, what allowed him to transcend fans' indifference toward the ditch-digging tough guys, was that in spite of his physical prowess, he seemed familiar, perhaps even fraternal. Goodridge is eminently likable: his blue-collar, working-class reputation and genuine assessments of his personal failings — from fatherhood to fidelity — humanize him in a way few fighters permit. During his prime, and even after it, many fans found it easy to imagine working at the auto plant with Goodridge, shooting the breeze in the break room. Something about Goodridge becoming a famous prizefighter feels democratic, like we all had a say in choosing one of our own to have that kind of success.

By chance, Gary Goodridge was present at several crucial junctions in MMA history, from the human cockfighting era to the dark ages of the UFC to the rise of MMA in Japan, the rivalry between K-1 and MMA, and today's sprawling, global climate in which a torn-up veteran might see the value in fighting on long past his prime. Goodridge helped transform the role of the gatekeeper in MMA and define what it meant to be a mid-card action fighter. With reckless abandon, he has found his way onto the winning and losing sides of highlight reels for generations to come, a conscious choice that now bears its vicious aftermath. The career of "Big Daddy" has been brutal, both for better and for worse.

Jordan Breen, January 2011

CHAPTER ONE

I am the little guy, the ditch digger, the farmer, the construction worker; I worked in a factory for many years, and every time I fight, I fight for those guys. I represent the heart and courage it takes for every average guy to get up in the morning and face another day. I represent the guys who take that shit-kicking and come home at the end of the day an accomplished person.

In late 2003, I was 37 years old and one of the most well-known mixed martial artists in the world. As the "Gatekeeper" of the Pride Fighting Championship's heavyweight division in Japan, I had fought the biggest, toughest, and most skilled heavyweights in the world. I didn't always win, but even when I lost, I always gave the fans an entertaining show. If I had been a cautious fighter, guarding my win-loss ratio like it was the last piece of cheesecake in the fridge, I'd look a lot better on paper. But I don't fight that way. In the era I was from, it didn't matter if you were a technical fighter, skilled in all of the various disciplines. The only thing the fans expected was that you fight with heart and keep going no matter what. Somebody's going to go home with a loss but at the end of the day, if you fought your heart out, you earned respect. My biggest worry going into the ring was always that I might disappoint my fans.

Despite my success, fighting had taken its toll on my personal life. Not only was the mother of my daughter Trinity harassing me for more money in child support payments, she was also pushing to keep my daughter full-time. That meant I would have only been able to see her every other weekend. My ex-girlfriend and I had shared custody, but all of a sudden, out of nowhere, she wanted full custody; she didn't think I was in the country enough. The only reason I fought in the first place was to feed my children and give them a better life; if my career was getting in the way of my relationship with my kids, then maybe it was time to start thinking about retirement.

It wasn't just the personal problems that were forcing me to get out. My body was beaten down from so many exciting but brutal fights throughout the years. Among other injuries, I had torn the cartilage in my knees, broken multiple fingers, cracked my ribs, lost several teeth, and had 30 stitches put above my eyebrow from a head kick that left me with a gaping wound. I was also suffering from a recurring back problem that stemmed from a car accident I had been in as a teenager. Every now and then, the pain would hit me like a wave, and near the end of 2003, the pain was particularly bad.

One afternoon, I was lying in bed in complete agony when I got a call from Nobuyuki Sakakibara, president of Dreamstage Entertainment, the Japanese-based company that owned Pride. Sakakibara had an interesting proposal: he wanted me to fight Don Frye on New Year's Eve, at the Saitama Super Arena in Japan. Don "The Predator" Frye looks like Tom Selleck and has a similar, really deep, gruff voice. Originally, Frye had been a firefighter but in 1994 he left the fire department to pursue a full-time career in mixed martial arts. When he started in the sport at UFC 8, Don Frye was already a former pro boxer and a second-degree black belt in judo with over 700 competition victories. He was also a stellar wrestler, having been state champion in high school and an all-American Greco-Roman and freestyle wrestler with Arizona State and Oklahoma State. Even though I had been bedridden for a month, I immediately knew that I wanted the fight. Earlier in my career, when I was still competing in the United States for the Ultimate Fighting Championship (UFC), Don had defeated me on two separate occasions. In those fights Frye had beaten me with experience and superior wrestling, but that had been eight years ago. Now that I also had experience, I was sure that I could beat Frye and avenge those two losses.

I wanted to fight Frye, but before I could do so I needed a new contract with Pride. The only thing that would keep me in the fight game was a pay raise and some guaranteed fights. That way I would be able to give my daughters more money in child support. I was in tremendous physical pain, but I knew I could fight if it meant a better future for my family. It had been almost a year since my last contract, and I wanted Pride to renew it or let me go. When I told Sakakibara I needed a contract extension or else I wouldn't fight, he quickly tried to change the subject, telling me we would talk about it another time. I was insistent; I needed an answer.

Sakakibara knew I wasn't going to budge, so he told me he needed to talk to some of the other Pride executives about renewing my contract. He called back a few times, but we couldn't agree on any of the terms he kept offering. Finally I got sick of it and told him not to call me back until he had made a decision that was fair. A short while later, Sakakibara called with his final offer: my fight against Don Frye would be my retirement fight, and Pride would give me $100,000, win or lose. Since I was thinking about retirement anyway, it sounded good to me. I'd make a lot of money, have a big retirement fight, and hopefully avenge my earlier losses to Frye.

Going into Pride Shockwave 2003 on New Year's Eve, there was no doubt in my mind that Don Frye was going to take a beating from me. Even with all of the personal problems and injuries I was dealing with, I was still confident that I was going to kick Frye's ass. He had been away from the game for a number of years doing professional wrestling in Japan, so I knew he wasn't at the top of his game. If I couldn't beat Frye at this point in our careers, I never would. There was no way I could allow myself to lose. Looking back, I didn't have many reasons to be so confident, but as a fighter, you can't allow doubt into your mind if you want to win.

During the trip over to Japan, I was in terrible pain. I could barely walk — the flight attendant had to keep bringing me ice packs. Backstage at the Saitama Super Arena, my back was still killing me. In order to try and get some mobility, I had one of the doctors shoot numbing agents into the muscles of my lower back. That helped for awhile. I used the respite from the pain to stretch out really well and throw a couple of high kicks at my assistant, Andrew McMichael, who was holding the pads. Due to my chronic injuries, that little bit of warming up was the only training I was able to do in the lead-up to the fight.

Frye was clearly having mobility problems of his own. Whenever he saw me looking, he'd jump up out of his seat as if there was nothing wrong. However, I could tell that just getting out of his chair was causing him a lot of pain. Don and I were both playing the game. Fighters always have to put their best foot forward. When you're going into battle, you want everybody to believe that you're functioning at full strength. Another option is to pretend you are a wimp, then come out there like a killer, but you have to be in control. In poker, you don't want somebody to see your hand before you show it. The same thing is true in fighting; despite appearances, it's largely a mental game.

When it was finally time to fight, I jogged and shadowboxed from my dressing room, down the main corridor leading into the arena, trying to loosen up. Emerging onto the long entrance ramp, I tried to stay calm as the crowd roared with anticipation. "We Will Rock You" by Queen came on, a laser light show started, and I began walking toward the ring. Along the way I pumped my fist in the air to the beat of the song, trying to block out all the other noise. Fighters who get caught up in all of the hoopla before a fight waste a lot of energy. You have to find a quiet, calm place in your mind. You don't want to be mesmerized by all of the fans wishing you well and cheering you on. To most people I looked calm, but the fact that I hadn't trained before the fight made me scared as hell. I really needed to focus my energy and try to overcome my nerves if I was going to beat Frye. At 6'1", 216 pounds, Don Frye was a very lean, tough guy. I concentrated on my strategy: I knew I had to keep the fight standing, because even after working for years on my grappling, Frye still had the advantage on the ground. There were a lot of things running through my mind before the fight but I tried to harness my adrenaline and use it to my advantage instead of letting it become a problem.

After an intense stare down with Frye during the announcements, I grabbed the back of his neck in a gesture of respect. Rather than reciprocating, Frye pushed me away and aggressively raised his gloves. I guess he was letting me know we could only be friends *after* the fight; right now, we had to go to war. When the bell rang, the crowd roared, and Frye and I touched gloves. He came out swinging, but I backed out of the way and hit him with a hard outside low kick to try and make him think twice about wading in with wild punches. I stalked Frye around the ring and loaded up on a big one-two combination that rocked him pretty hard. When he tried to clinch, I pushed him away then stalked after him, hitting him with a hard left hook.

I took a brief pause and assessed the situation: Frye's background was wrestling and wrestlers are susceptible to being kicked in the head because they tend to keep their hands low. At that moment, Frye dropped his hands slightly, so I loaded up my right leg for a huge kick to the side of his head. The kick landed perfectly and knocked Frye out cold, sending him face down on the mat. When Frye hit the floor, the Japanese fans went absolutely crazy and gave me a huge standing ovation. It was a fantastic feeling. As Stephen Quadros, the announcer for Pride, said on the broadcast, Hollywood could not have scripted a better ending for my career. Nor could I have asked for a better opponent to fight. Don Frye had been so significant in my mixed martial arts life because he had beaten me twice in my first year as a pro fighter. A win over him was a hurdle I had to clear, and the perfect ending to a long and turbulent career.

After a short celebration in the ring, I went over to make sure Frye was all right. From the mat, he winked at me as if to say, "Yeah, you got me," then sat up and gave me a hug. Next, the Pride head honchos, Nobuhiko Takada and Sakakibara, came in and gave me a giant trophy, two big bouquets of flowers, and my money. When Sakakibara told me to keep in touch, all I could manage to say in response was "Thank you. Thank you for all of the wonderful years." Takada called me "Mr. Pride," which was a huge honor for me: at the time, Pride was the best mixed martial arts organization in the world. Once Frye was up and walking around, he held up my hand with the trophy in it. Frye was my nemesis, but he was also a brother of mine in the art of war. We had started in the game at the exact same time.

My final fight was a really emotional time for me and as I hugged my team in the ring, the tears started to flow. I can't even describe the rush of emotions I was feeling. When given the microphone to address the crowd, I said *"Sumimasen,"* which means "I'm sorry." "I'm really emotional," I continued, "because tonight means a lot to me. Thank you to all my Japanese fans for making me feel at home every time I come here." After my words were translated, the crowd cheered. I didn't want to stay in the ring all night, so I wished everybody a happy new year and left the ring to continue the celebration backstage. For a moment, everything was gone: the pain, the problems, the worries about what to do next — all of it. But just for a moment. Even at what I thought was the end of my career, it soon became clear my life would continue to be what it had been from the start: a fight.

CHAPTER TWO

I was born in Saint James, Trinidad, on January 17, 1966, to Henry and Barbara Goodridge. In the old country, my parents were extremely poor, so we lived in a really small dwelling. How poor were we? I remember going to school some mornings with no breakfast and then barely being able to afford to spend the little bit of money that it cost for lunch. Discipline was strict and harsh, and I had to deal with a lot of beatings whenever I misbehaved. In Trinidad, if you did something you weren't supposed to do, you got beat for it. My mother and father used to work extremely long hours, which meant that us kids were usually left on our own. Even when my dad wasn't working, he wasn't around because he was usually off fooling around with somebody.

My sisters and I spent a lot of time at my grandparents' place a few streets away. If we weren't at home, my mom would march over to my grandparents' place with a belt and start beating us, even if we were sleeping — she didn't like to have to chase us down after a long day. There were lots of times we'd have to quickly grab our clothes and run down the street while my mom ran after us, threatening bodily harm and yelling, "Get out of here! You're supposed to be at home!" For a young kid, getting woken up like that was pretty scary. However, it got me used to taking a beating, something that would come in handy later on in my life.

After years living in poverty, my parents decided that they wanted a better life for their kids so they started the process of immigrating to Canada. Like many immigrants, we couldn't afford to move the whole family at once, so my father moved first to set up living arrangements and start making money. The plan was that once my father established himself, the rest of the family would move to the new country one by one, as we could afford it. Approximately one year after my father left, my mother joined him in Toronto. For two years my younger sister Susie and I lived with my mother's father in Barbados. (My sisters Sharon and Shirma left for Canada after a year in Barbados.) He was a painter by trade. He was also an alcoholic and would stay up and talk all night, telling stories about his childhood or singing old war tunes until he had sung himself to sleep.

Being left behind by my parents gave me a fear of being abandoned. People make comments like, "Your parents left you in a nice tropical island like Barbados? How bad could that be?!" But it's not like that. My parents left me at a very young and vulnerable age when people could have taken advantage of me. Nobody looks after you as much as your parents do. Even today, leaving is one of the worst things that anybody could do to me. It's an awful feeling that I have experienced many times throughout my life. When somebody who you love leaves you, it always feels like the entire world is falling apart.

I have four sisters: Susie, Shirma, Sharon, and Lisa. They are the backbone of who I am. Throughout my life I have had many relationships. Many people have come and gone, but I can't divorce my family; they are a part of me forever. As the middle child between two older sisters and two younger sisters, I have always been spoiled. My sister Shirma is just like my mom in a lot of ways: an outspoken person and a fighter. Shirma was the one who always fought my battles if I was being bullied. Even to this day, if anyone messes around with me, they better prepare to mess with Shirma and my mom.

Although I love all of my sisters to death, Susie and I have always had a particularly special bond. Ever since Susie and I were left by ourselves at such a young age, we have never been apart from one another. When everybody else in our family was splitting up, we were always kept together. As a result, we've always been there for each other. One day my mom went into the bank, leaving Susie and me in the car to look after our younger sister Lisa. At the time, Lisa was just a little snotty-nosed kid; Susie and I were starting to get fed up with taking her everywhere that we went. This particular day, Lisa was nagging me non-stop and just being a pain in the testicles. Finally, I'd had enough, and since I couldn't hit her, I turned around and spit in her face. The minute the spit hit her, she started screaming like somebody was trying to kill her. I began to worry about what my mom was going to do to me: was I going to get kicked out of the house?

When my mom got back in the car and asked why Lisa was being so hysterical, I was prepared for the worst. However, Susie piped up and said, "I don't know what happened, Mom. Lisa's lying: Gary didn't spit on her." Instead of getting me in trouble, my mom slapped Lisa and told her to behave. Even more satisfying than getting off the hook was the fact that Susie stuck up for me. It was the kind of relationship we still have.

• • •

When I first moved to Canada at the age of seven, I had a lot of problems adjusting to the new culture. Part of the reason was because I wasn't sure who I was. My family had been separated for so long, I couldn't even remember my dad at all, and I only had a few vague memories of my mom. I'd never seen so many white people before in my life. When I was growing up in Trinidad and Barbados, I thought the world was only as big as my block. As soon as I landed in Canada, I realized that wasn't the case.

I remember my first Christmas in Canada being pretty strange because Santa had been so different in the old country. In Trinidad, there was this guy who would dress up in a Santa suit and buy toys for all of the kids in the district. He would drive around to all the houses with a bunch of pretty women dressed up as his little elves. Of course, I was too young to really pay attention to the girls back then; I just wanted the toys. When Santa got to your house in Trinidad, he used to dance and sing, and it was always a lot of fun. In Canada, Santa didn't sing or dance; he just sat on a chair in the mall and took pictures with kids. It wasn't just that Santa acted differently in Canada, he even *looked* different. All of my life Santa had been a black man, but when I came to Canada, he was white. For a child, that was a huge thing. I was devastated and couldn't wrap my brain around it. It was an eye-opener.

My family only lived in Toronto for about a year before moving to Barrie, a small city approximately an hour's drive north. I remember being terrified walking into class on my first day at Steele Street Public School. The teacher asked someone in the class to show me around, and a friendly white kid named Mike Mobbs volunteered to give me the tour. From that moment on, Mike and I have been best friends. He and I were virtually inseparable. Along with going for tours on our bikes all over the city, we used to play a lot of video games. Mike had nearly all of the early video game systems like Atari and Intellivision, so we used to play at his house all the time. Our favorite was Atari's *Pong*. Mike's dad was the master at all of the games, and we could never beat him. However, that didn't stop us from spending hours trying. We also played a lot of basketball together because he had a net in his driveway. Mike would always kick my ass at basketball and he probably still can. For the most part, we were just ordinary kids.

Because there was a lot of arguing at home and my father made it uncomfortable to be there, I tried to be there as little as possible. Mike was a cadet and used to be away every year for the entire summer, which left me at home alone. With Mike gone, the summers seemed to drag on forever. Four or five summers in a row I just played by myself, a lost puppy. I tried joining the cadets in order to be with Mike and go on all of their outings, but I quickly discovered that being a cadet was not my thing. I don't even think I lasted an entire year before quitting.

Growing up, Mike and I were like brothers, and we were always looking after each other. Neither one of us ever smoked or did drugs, so we didn't have to put up with the type of peer pressure that some of the other kids did. (It may be hard for anyone to believe but I was even an altar boy at church, helping the priest give Holy Communion.) Our goal for when we were older was to work together as police detectives in the same cruiser. We were basically just two nerds who hung out and had a good time. I can probably count on one hand the amount of times we did stupid things that most kids get in trouble for.

Even when we did party, Mike and I came across as pretty straight kids. In high school we went out drinking one time with a Welsh rugby team that'd just beaten our own. I wasn't used to alcohol, so by the end of the night I could barely walk. According to Mike, I was passed out in the back seat of the car on the way home and I started crying. There I was, this huge 200-pound guy, and I was sobbing about how I missed my mom and how she was going to be mad at me.

On that first day of school in Barrie I also met the first woman I ever fell in love with: Noreen Virgin, one of my first teachers. As a black woman, Mrs. Virgin honed in right away on the type of help that I needed, which is what I think the school had in mind when they paired us up. Barrie was predominately white and middle class, and I stood out like a fly in a bowl of milk.

Mrs. Virgin took me under her wing and helped steer me along. Because she wasn't afraid to discipline me if I stepped out of line, I both loved and hated her. One day I'd tell Mrs. Virgin that I wanted to marry her. The next, she might discipline me for something I had done wrong, and I wouldn't want anything to do with her. Mrs. Virgin drove me nuts and to this day I still have a soft spot for her. I don't know how anybody could adjust to a brand new culture without somebody like her guiding them.

Mrs. Virgin had a daughter named Yvette who was the same age as me and went to the same school. In grades four, five, and six, she was my nemesis, and we used to bicker and fight all of the time. Yvette was mixed-race, so we both stood out from all of the other kids in Barrie. Even though we had that in common, Yvette and I were combatants. She was a tomboy and bigger than most of the other kids our age, so we were always challenging each other. I remember I used to tell people that when I grew up, I was going to marry Mrs. Virgin and kick Yvette out of the house.

Ever since I was really young I always spent my spare time working. My first job was as a paperboy. After that I worked jobs at places like Harper's Pharmacy, Burger King, the cinema, and Maud Currie's Steakhouse. When I was 18 years old, I got a part-time bouncing job at a club in Barrie called the Blue Lagoon. At the time, I was sleeping with a girl on a regular basis who was about eight years older than me. While I checked IDs and worked the door, she sat beside me. At the end of the night, she would give me a ride home and we would have sex in her car.

One night, she came into the bar with one of her friends and asked me if I had any place that the three of us could go. At first I had to say no because I was still living with my parents, so we definitely couldn't go to my house. The wheels in my head started turning; there was *no way* I could pass up an opportunity like this. The Blue Lagoon was also a motel, so I went upstairs and stole a key to one of the rooms. After the bar closed, the two girls and I waited until everyone else had left the club. Then we went up into the room. There I was, only 18 years old, having sex with two ladies. It was a big eye-opener.

Around four in the morning, we heard somebody trying to open the door. We all jumped up and quickly tried to grab our clothes in the dark. On the other side of the door was a 50-year-old man who had rented out the room for the night. Realizing that there were people in the room, he apologized. "Oh I'm sorry," he said. "I thought this room was mine for the night. I must have gotten the wrong key."

As soon as he left I told the girls we had to go, and quickly. There wasn't even time to put on all of our clothes. We just grabbed our stuff and rushed out into the hall. As we were leaving we ran into Blanche, the lady who worked at the front desk and rented out the rooms. "Gary, what are you doing in there?!" she screamed. "Give me that key and get outta here!"

The next day I got called into the boss's office. Right away, he asked me what the hell I had been doing. I knew there was no point in lying so I decided to tell the truth. "Well," I said, "I had an opportunity to have a threesome and I didn't have a place to go because I live with my parents." My boss thought about what I said for what seemed like an eternity. Then he looked me straight in the eye and said, "Well, don't do that again. We can't be doing those kinds of things at work." He said it firmly but was smiling the whole time. I knew what that meant: "Don't do it again . . . but good for you."

Because I'm a professional fighter, people assume I must have gotten in a lot of fights when I was a kid. The truth is, the only physical fighting I did growing up was wrestling with my sisters and my cousin Hazel, who used to live with us. Hazel, my father's niece, was brought into our family hastily because Hazel's mom didn't have her immigration papers together. My parents eventually adopted her. Hazel lived with us for a long time, but she moved to the U.S. as an adult; I haven't seen her since. She was a pretty well-built kid and older than me, and she used to beat the crap out of me all the time. Other than that, I never really got into any schoolyard fights or confrontations. I was always too afraid that I was going to kill somebody and get in a lot of trouble. I always thought that if I hit someone, they would disappear.

Since other kids recognized that I was not very aggressive, I got bullied a lot. Everyone has a block bully when they're a kid and mine was a guy named Paul Winnegar. Paul lived up the street from me on Bernick Drive; he bullied just about everybody on the block. I first came onto Paul's radar when I was about 10 years old. Paul was only a few years older than me, but at that age, a few years' difference was huge. I was a kid, and Paul seemed almost man-sized. He even had a beard and a mustache — or at least it seemed like it at the time. In reality, he probably only had peach fuzz. Either way, it was more than I had.

I used to walk home from school with my sisters and that was when Paul would terrorize me. He'd chase me around, tackle me, then beat me up. Of course, at that age, getting beat up meant getting pushed in the snow, sat on, and maybe smacked around a few times. I never retaliated. Susie always ran home to tell my mother what happened. When I got home, I would usually get another beating from my mom for letting somebody bully me. My mom's beatings were even more brutal; she is quick-tempered, and her hands were fast. In order for me to stop getting the double beating, I had to beat Paul. My parents used to say, "This guy's the same size as you. Just beat him!" Of course I *wanted* to beat Paul at the time, I just didn't understand how I could possibly fight somebody three or four years older than me.

One day I came home after school crying and out of breath. Paul had beaten me up again by the corner store. My mom was sick of it, so she ordered me to get my jacket on: we were going to find him. I started to cry even harder because I really didn't want to go. I was praying that Paul would not still be there.

When my mother, Susie, and I finally got to the corner store, Paul was still sitting there on his 10-speed bike. My mom told me to go and get him. I was devastated, but I had no choice. As I approached Paul, he just stood there, frozen. He wouldn't do anything because my mother and sister were right behind me. That's when my mom started cheering me on, saying, "Hit him, Gary. Hit him!" I ended up kicking Paul, throwing him to the ground, and smacking him around a little bit. Then I started to ease up because I didn't want Paul to retaliate the next day when my mom and sister were not around. Back then I didn't understand the way the human psyche works. Now I know that what I needed to do was put a good enough ass-whooping on Paul that he wouldn't even think of coming after me again. My mom knew that

Paul wasn't getting seriously hurt and told me to keep hitting him — she wanted to make sure she wouldn't have to deal with a crying kid anymore. To appease my mom, I kind of tapped Paul around just a little bit more until I could tell that he had taken enough punishment.

I thought my problems with Paul Winnegar were over, but a few weeks later, he started to bully me again. This time, my mother really wanted to teach him a lesson, so she gave me a thick wire extension cord, about an inch in diameter. She told me, "If you see Paul, pull out the wire and show him you have it. If he comes at you, take the wire, wrap it around your hand, and start to swing it around like you're crazy."

I didn't see Paul for a while, but one day I ran into him with some girls, and he started getting mouthy. I pulled the extension cord out of my pocket and smacked him across the legs as hard as I could. *Whack. Whack. Whack. Whack. Whack.* He started rolling around on the ground, crying like a baby, and I ran back home to tell my mom. That afternoon at school, the police called me out of class to charge me with beating up Paul. My parents and I ended up going to court over the incident, and we even needed to put a lien on the house just to be able to cover the court costs. It came out in court that Paul was a block bully whom I'd been trying to teach a lesson. My mother told the judge, "I didn't bring my kids here for anybody to abuse them. My kids were taught never to hit first, but I also taught them not to let anybody bully them."

• • •

My entire life, through all the ups and downs, my mom has always been a rock for my sisters and me. My mom is a working woman, a hustler. If there weren't any jobs, my mom would find a job. If there wasn't anything to eat, she would find something to eat. My mom always pushed herself. She went to college and upgraded her book-keeping skills, while at the same time running her own ceramics craft company and delivering papers with the kids. Canadians will sometimes ask my mom why she came to this country; it gets her upset because she is more Canadian than most of the people who are asking. My mom *chose* to come here. She takes a lot of pride in the fact that she put her hand on the Bible and swore allegiance to this country. A lot of people didn't have to do that because they just happened to be born here.

My mom was the engine that propelled everything in our family. She instilled proper values in my sisters and me. She stressed that we must try to achieve and succeed. My mother was always going forward, never sitting still. My mother never left a stone unturned in her efforts to improve. She had the drive to succeed and she passed that desire along to her children. She was our main supporter and provider growing up. She got cleaning contracts at night and would take us with her to help clean offices. We also delivered bundles of newspapers twice a week at five a.m. for the *Barrie Banner*. My mom drove the van around and the kids would be counting out the papers and dropping off the bundles.

In the early part of my career, my mom had a big problem with me being a fighter, refusing to even watch me fight. However, there comes a time when parents have to let their kids go, and my mom ended up cheering me on and encouraging me in the fight game. Thankfully, because of my success, I've been able to pay my mother back for some of the things she's done for me. Charity starts at home, and I'm happy that I could buy her some vehicles and help her out here and there over the years.

Unlike my mom, my dad was a bum. He had no drive to succeed or achieve. He tried to instill the importance of hard work in our brains, but he could never back it up with his actions. My mom would say it and then do it.

All the same, I thought of my dad as a good man and a good friend. He tried to be a good father, but I think his own upbringing stopped him. My dad never had anybody to help bring him up, so he ended up raising himself. Because of that, my father had a lot of emotional issues that never got taken care of. Men don't talk about things like that; they just try to forget about their problems. My dad had issues that he needed to resolve, but he never did. In retrospect, that's probably why my dad was more of a friend to me than a father.

CHAPTER THREE

Other than Mike, I didn't have a lot of friends growing up, which is probably because I've never been much of a party animal. I didn't smoke. I didn't drink. I didn't do recreational drugs of any sort. I was only into working out and improving my body, and I didn't want to put anything in my body that I didn't think would make me a better person.

I was always big for my age, so I usually played sports with older kids. I used to think that I was strong then but looking back, I realize I wasn't. Plus, my growth spurts made me clumsy. However, when I reached my teenage years, I started working out, gaining muscle, and becoming more coordinated. I played football and rugby every year in high school, and, like every good Canadian kid, I even tried playing rinky-dink Legion hockey for a couple of years. I was a standout on the defensive line in football but also played offence. Whenever my team got within 10 yards of the opponent's goal line, the coaches would call me in to do the Marcus Allen–type thing and power it in for the touchdown.

I was always good at every sport I tried, but I was never great. I was still searching for a sport that I could excel at. Gradually, I realized I didn't like team sports very much, preferring one-on-one sports where if you lose, you have no one to blame but yourself. The first sport that earned me any real success and recognition was arm-wrestling. I used to arm-wrestle my dad a lot. In fact, my first real physical challenge in life was trying to beat my dad. As a kid I wasn't much of a match for my dad who was over six feet tall and probably close to 300 pounds. My dad used to wrestle me with one finger — his finger was the size of my wrist. I never did end up getting a victory over my dad; when I was finally big enough and strong enough to beat him, he wouldn't face me anymore.

Around the age of 15, I got involved in the local arm-wrestling scene in Barrie. I started out training and competing on Monster arm-wrestling machines, which basically looked like bicycle handlebars, one for each opponent to hold on to. Pretty soon, I was beating all challengers. One night, I was walking around downtown with my cousin Garvin and a friend of ours from Jamaica. Garvin and I were just messing around and trying to speak in a Jamaican patois, when all of a sudden this white guy who was walking in front of us turned around and started talking to us in patois. Garvin and I looked at each other with bewilderment, thinking, *What the hell?! He's talking better Jamaican than we are . . . and he's white!* It turned out his name was Phil Stoppart, and he was a well-known puller within the local arm-wrestling circuit.

Phil was excited when he found out that I was also an arm-wrestler. Since he had more experience than me, he took me under his wing and helped me make the most of my abilities. Until I met Phil, I was only successful because of my sheer physical strength. I had been lifting weights since I was 14 years old and within a few years had won local weightlifting challenges. At the peak of my muscular strength I was benching 585 pounds. When I lifted weights, everybody in the gym would stop and look at me. More impressive than my bench press, in my opinion, was my military press — when you lift the barbell to shoulder height in one motion and then lift it overhead in another. I used to be able to military press 405 pounds and, to this day, the strongest part of me is my shoulders. I was also curling 225 pounds for 12 repetitions, doing them on the preacher's bench, which was great for arm-wrestling because it developed good back muscles. Good back muscles lead to better back pressure which you need to develop in order to jerk your opponent away from where he gets the most power. In my prime I could also do chin-ups with just my right arm, an extremely rare ability. I could do 32 chin-ups in 30 seconds and nearly a hundred push-ups in a minute. At its biggest, my bicep measured as 19 3/4 inches, without pumping it up.

My strength was certainly a huge asset, but Phil Stoppart told me that if I really wanted to learn how to arm-wrestle properly, I should go and watch some arm-wrestling tournaments and see what I was getting myself into. Phil had been free-hand arm-wrestling for five years, which was much more technical and difficult than the Monster arm-wrestling I was used to. He was a naturally strong guy, and he was always beating guys bigger and older than him. In fact, when Phil and I first met, I thought for sure I would be able to beat him. However, when we finally sat down and had a free-hand arm-wrestling match, he kicked my ass. I was shocked: Phil was the first person to beat me in a long time. I quickly learned that superior technique can overcome a strength advantage. It was an important lesson, and there were more to come.

Phil wasn't greedy with the knowledge that he had attained. Instead, he tried to make everyone around him better. He was good at woodworking and built an arm-wrestling table in his garage. Every week he would invite people to come practice and improve. It quickly became a sort of arm-wrestling club. One thing Phil always stressed to us was that you have to pull your opponents hand toward you before you start "going over." It is a crucial maneuver inexperienced pullers usually forget.

When Phil and I started arm-wrestling, it was hard to learn the techniques because nobody wanted to share their secrets. Phil and I would watch people and figure out how to do it ourselves. It's not like today where there are arm-wrestling clubs with everybody helping to teach everybody else. Back then it was just Phil and me against everybody else. It took Phil nine years to win his first Canadian title. It's different today.

I was strong and I learned fast. With Phil's help I developed better technique, and it wasn't long before I could beat Phil — and everyone else I faced — at a local hangout in Barrie called Wizards. My friends and family were amazed at how quickly I began to dominate at arm-wrestling, but it shouldn't have come as such a surprise — I had all of the attributes that a puller needs to become a champion. Along with the natural gifts of being very strong and agile, I am quite versatile and can change up the game plan midstream. More importantly, I have always been eager to learn and driven to win. Often arm-wrestling comes down to muscle stamina and who wants it more. Some contests only last a fraction of a second, while others might go for over eight minutes. At that point it becomes more of a mental challenge than a physical one. Arm-wrestling is more about technique than size. It's about who moves faster from the start and who is able to carry through to the end.

One of my first free-hand wins in an actual tournament happened when I was 17 years old and competing at an outdoor festival close to my hometown. At the time I weighed 179 pounds, but I signed up for the 181–200 pound weight class because I didn't want to wrestle Phil or my cousin Garvin. Even though I was outsized, I ended up winning both my own weight class and the left-handed open weight class, which garnered me some attention in the local press. A year later I won my first Canadian Arm-wrestling Championship at the convention centre in Toronto by beating a Toronto-based puller named "Jungle" Jay Martin. Many top Canadian pullers were astounded that I had walked into the national arm-wrestling scene and immediately become so highly ranked. I was the envy of all of the other arm-wrestlers. Some guys arm-wrestled for 10 to 15 years before reaching my level. However, it wasn't as if I hadn't earned my ranking. Even at an early age, my motto was "practice makes perfect." Every day, I would practice for two hours on an arm-wrestling table at my house. It may not have taken me as long as some others, but I still paid my dues.

During my early arm-wrestling days, Phil would always drive me around to the different regional tournaments, which I was really appreciative of. Whenever I would make some money from those tournaments I'd try to give Phil half for driving me there. He always refused to take it, however, telling me I was "too generous" because I had been the one to earn it. Phil ended up winning five Canadian titles and the 1993 world title. Once I had really made a name for myself in arm-wrestling, I managed to get some sponsors, which allowed Phil and me to travel to tournaments all around North America for a couple of years. Due to my constant willingness to travel and compete, I really came into my own during that time and just completely took over the sport. For a while I was crushing everybody I faced, making me a marked man.

· · ·

At the same time that I was tearing up the national arm-wrestling circuit, I was still going to school and working part-time as a bouncer. As a bouncer I could meet girls and make some easy money over the weekend. Bouncing also gave me a chance to sharpen my fighting skills, which would come in handy later on in my life. When I first started bouncing at the age of 18, I was really intimidated by the idea of trying to kick people out who were almost twice my age. I was certainly big for an 18-year-old, but I was still just a kid. If a well-seasoned street fighter had started a confrontation with me, they would have picked up on my fear right away. I wasn't intimidated by others for very long, though. After bouncing for a few years, I even started developing confidence in my ability to intimidate others. For people who like to fight, being a bouncer is the perfect job, because a fight is bound to happen. Most of the time, bouncers are just *dying* for something to happen so that they can fight somebody.

One night I was working at a bar in Barrie, and the other bouncers and I were just itching for a fight. At some point during the night, Phil came in with another friend of his whom I had never met before. Phil and I chatted for a bit, but I didn't pay much attention to the guy he had come in with. About an hour after Phil arrived, some drunk started acting like an idiot. The other bouncers and I did what we did to every other drunken idiot: we kicked him out. We roughed him up for a little bit and then threw him out onto the street.

Five minutes later the same guy came back to the door and waved a finger at me to come over. I walked over to the door and stuck my head out to listen to what this guy had to say, and this idiot sucker-punched me as hard as he could. Dizzy as hell, it was all I could do to reach out and grab the guy by his shirt.

As I was grabbing this guy, trying to get my bearings, my friend Bob and my cousin Garvin came running over and started kicking and punching him as hard as they could, just going to town on him. When I finally let the guy go, he was a bloody mess, and we figured that was the end of it. However, this guy wasn't going to let it go without fighting one of us again. Since the other two had already fought him, I wanted a turn. I wanted to pay him back for the sucker punch, and pay him back I did. I bounced this guy all over the pavement. I mean, literally: I kept picking him up and throwing him down on the pavement.

In the middle of all this, Phil came out of the bar. Apparently the drunk guy we had been beating up was the same friend he had come into the bar with. He took one look at his bloodied friend and lost it on me. Phil stayed mad at me for a while after that; it was the only time there has ever been any animosity between us throughout our friendship. Eventually he figured out that his friend had only gotten a beating because he had sucker-punched me first.

A few years later I was working as a bouncer at another bar in Barrie called the Continental. While I was checking IDs at the back door, this guy came up and started causing a scene. I'm not exactly sure what his deal was — he wasn't overly drunk, just an obnoxious idiot. I didn't let him in. He went around the other side of the club to try and get in another door, but the other bouncers spotted him and came to the same conclusion I did: *no way*. After getting turned away again, the guy came back around to my door and started yapping to the people coming into the bar telling them, "Don't go in there. They're all a bunch of idiots." No one likes being bothered and it wasn't too long before this guy ended up getting into a bit of a scuffle with somebody before taking off.

The manager, whose family owned the club, came up to me and some other bouncers and said, "Grab that guy." I wanted to be the first guy to catch him, so I raced out of the door ahead of everybody else. As I got close he did a buttonhook turn, which left me slipping through the wet grass in my brand new shoes. By the time I brushed myself off and ran over to the other bouncers, they had already caught the troublemaker and had him propped up on the fence, trying to push him over. They weren't tall enough or strong enough to pitch him all the way over, so I gave this guy an extra shove, slam dunking him over the fence. He hit the ground hard, then got up slowly and then started yelling at us: "You bastards! You fucking assholes! You niggers!" There were only two black guys there at the time.

Everybody had a good laugh about it on the way back to the club, and the night just continued on. A little while later, I saw a car slowing down and quickly stopping on the highway next to the club. It had its four-way emergency lights on. After that another car on the highway stopped and put its four-ways on. Then a third car stopped. By this point, the commotion on the highway had caught everyone's attention.

One of the bouncers decided to jump over the fence and find out what was going on. A few minutes later he ran back into the club, almost out of breath. "You know that guy we threw over the fence?!" he asked. "He's all over the highway! . . . He's dead!" As soon as I heard those words, my stomach dropped and my mind started racing. Immediately I was wondering how much I was at fault and whether or not I was going to end up in jail.

Highway 400 was closed down for the next 16 hours as the police tried to sort out what had happened. The police checked the guy's blood alcohol level to make sure he hadn't been drunk or on drugs when we had thrown him over the fence. If he had been, it would have been like throwing a helpless child onto the highway; however, that wasn't the case. In the end, the judge ruled that we shouldn't have thrown him over the fence, but we weren't responsible for his death. The family of the deceased and their lawyers attacked the bar owner from all angles to try and get money for their family, which they absolutely should have. In the end, the family got nothing. It was an unfortunate situation for everybody, and I've always felt bad about them losing their son in such a tragic way.

. . .

With arm-wrestling and bouncing taking up most of my time, I didn't really have much of an interest in high school, which caused a few problems with the vice-principal of my school, Mr. Lloyd Preston. During my senior year at Eastview Secondary, things between Mr. Preston and I came to a head at the school's year-end dance. One of the people I went to school with was a short, stocky guy named Antonio. Even though he was small, Antonio had vise-grip hands one-and-a-half times the size of mine. Every time we shook, he'd get the jump on me and crush my hand, forcing me to beg for mercy. At the dance I went up to him as soon as I saw him and put out my hand for a shake. I could tell Antonio thought he was going to get me again, but this time, I got the jump on him. I held on a little longer than I should have, because it was the first time I'd won any of those contests.

When Mr. Preston saw what was going on, he immediately came over and started yelling at me. As he was kicking me out of the dance, I started begging him to put his hands on me. "Please touch me," I pleaded. "Just put a hand on me so I can knock the piss out of you! Do anything wrong and I've got you." I gave Mr. Preston a tongue-lashing because, at that point in my life, I was completely fed up with school. I know I was an asshole and shouldn't have done it. My behavior toward my vice-principal was completely uncalled for, and I'm certainly not proud of it. Even though Mr. Preston seemed to have it out for me, he was a good man and he didn't deserve the earful he got from me. His job was to look after the students and when he saw me inflicting pain on someone, he had to stop it. After the incident at the dance, the school administrators wanted to expel me. Foolishly, I welcomed the expulsion, but the school board decided I didn't deserve to be expelled. Since there was very little time left in the school year, it was decided I would have to complete my final courses at home, which suited me just fine.

• • •

In 1986, at the age of 19, I heard about an upcoming contest called the Canadian Over-the-Top Arm-wrestling Competition. The tournament was being held for Sylvester Stallone's upcoming movie called *Over the Top*, about an underdog arm-wrestler. In order to bring some authenticity to the film, Sly decided to hold a series of national arm-wrestling competitions around the world. Each winner would receive $10,000, a chance to appear in the movie, and a trip to Las Vegas to compete in the international finals against the world's best arm-wrestlers. The Canadian Over-the-Top Tournament was held at the convention center in Toronto and featured about 200 of the nation's most accomplished pullers. The tournament was structured in a double-elimination style, which meant that each competitor had to lose twice in order to be out. I entered the 196–238 pound weight class at 227 pounds, making me one of the bigger competitors and an early favorite to win the tournament.

My first grapples were against good competitors, but I still ended up easily making it to the finals. I then faced off against a really top-notch national competitor named Rick Baarbe. Rick and I were long-time rivals and had already faced off against each other several times.

Baarbe, who is from Kitchener, Ontario, and about 10 years older than me, is a massive, burly man with a big, pushed-out belly and huge, powerful hands. Rick and I started off with two intense back-and-forth grapples that saw me win the first and him take the second. Going into the third and final grapple was a big moment for me. I knew that in order to beat Baarbe and win the tournament, I would have to step up mentally and become a man. I gave it everything I had from the beginning. It was a winning strategy and I flashed Baarbe in eight seconds, tearing some muscles in my arms and shoulders in the process. I knew it was a huge win for my career as a puller, and I was overjoyed. Although I couldn't move my arm for days after the tournament, it was definitely worth it.

A few months later, when I arrived at the Las Vegas Hilton for the filming of *Over the Top*, I was amazed at the size of the spectacle. Instead of setting up a fake arm-wrestling tournament, the producers of the movie had decided that they were going to film scenes for the movie during the actual competition. For that reason, many of the actors in *Over the Top* were legitimate world-class arm-wrestlers from all over the world, including Carl Adams, Rick Zumwalt, and Cleve Dean. The tournament was held in a massive room at the Hilton, but there were so many huge athletes around, the place was crammed. There were over 600 competitors and they were all mammoths. The smell in the room was thick with Absorbing Jr., Rub A535, and other topical analgesics. There were cameras shooting scenes all over the place and tons of people telling the crowds when it was time to scream and when it was time to cheer. All of the grapplers were set up on tables, and whenever the film's director, Menahem Golan, was ready for a certain shot, the movie crew would stick the actors in the middle of what was going on.

Walking around the area where the arm-wrestlers weigh in, I was just trying to digest everything that was going on around me. It was mind-boggling. I noticed Sly Stallone and his entourage, and looked on cynically as the other arm-wrestlers clamored to take a picture with the star like they were good friends. I was still a headstrong kid with too much ego to go up and ask Sly for a picture. At that point in my life, I felt like I would be lowering myself to go up to another man like that.

The international Over-the-Top double-elimination tournament took place over the course of nearly 24 hours. Arm-wrestlers slept on benches at the sides and then woke up and went to arm-wrestle when they heard their names called over the loudspeakers. The best arm-wrestlers, like John Brzenk, who ended up winning the tournament, competed in the open class for the chance at winning a truck. I was in the 220–242 pound heavyweight class, competing for a money prize.

In my first bout of the day I got beat by Gene Tatti, a 40-year-old arm-wrestling promoter from Ontario. I should have beaten Tatti, but since I didn't, I was in the loser's bracket right away. That meant that I had to be the best of the losers in order to win the whole tournament. After the loss to Tatti, I strung together a few winning grapples throughout the day until I finally ran into a guy named Rick Vardell. At first I thought they were saying "Rick Barbell" and thought, *What an appropriate name for an arm-wrestler.* . . . As soon as our grapple began, Rick Vardell manhandled me like a rag doll. His hands were like spiders and completely enveloped mine. As soon as the match started, Vardell drove me down in a top roll faster than I could blink. I couldn't even complain or protest because it was over so quickly. I was completely humiliated. Even though I came in sixth place out of hundreds of world-class competitors, my final pull against Rick Vardell turned out to be one of the toughest losses I have ever had. I had known about the Over-the-Top Tournament for a long time and I had worked so hard leading up to it. I never prepared myself for the possibility that I might lose, so when I did, it absolutely devastated me.

After I lost to Rick Vardell, I left the competition table and went straight to the bathroom. I didn't say anything to anybody. All I could do was sit down on some stairs in the bathroom and cry like a baby for about 40 minutes. I could barely even lift my head up because I was so weak with emotion. All of a sudden, this huge arm-wrestler from the super-heavyweight class came over and started patting me on the back like I was a little kid. In the sweetest voice, he asked, "What are you crying about? It's okay. I saw that you got sixth place. That's really good. You did well today!" Although it was a nice gesture for a stranger to try and comfort me, I felt like an even bigger idiot. I didn't need a therapist or a shoulder to cry on. I'm just very competitive at everything I do and I don't like getting beat. I don't even let my daughters win at board games.

Even though I was upset about my results at the tournament, I now look back at my experience there as a great time. I would never trade that memory for anything. It gave me a bit of the acting bug, and throughout my career I landed a few small movie roles. In 1995, I was cast as the "Angel of Death" in the movie *Gladiator Cop: The Swordsman II*, starring Lorenzo Lamas. I was also in the *Mortal Combat* movie, in a commercial for Sega Genesis as "Rogad," and played a bodyguard and fighter in a movie filmed in Toronto called *Khiladiyon Ka Khiladi*.

• • •

In October 1986, shortly after Over-the-Top, I won my first right-handed world arm-wrestling title at Sherway Gardens in Toronto. Although my first world title was a big deal, it didn't immediately make me a top-ranked competitor in the world arm-wrestling scene. That's because the sport of arm-wrestling is so unorganized and everybody has their own tournaments and world championships. Just because you call it a world championship doesn't mean that it features all of the top arm-wrestlers in the world. Regardless, my win at Sherway Gardens was my first big international title and I'm proud of it.

A year later I defeated Bobby Hopkins and Brad Silver to win another world championship in England. Bobby Hopkins is a former professional football player who is so massive I think he has muscles in his shit. Brad Silver is a giant biker-looking guy with massive shoulders. There was a picture in a magazine that Silver liked so much he wanted it tattooed on his arm; they were able to fit the entire full-size picture on his arm — that's how big it is. My first international win may not have earned much notice, but the wins over Hopkins and Silver definitely helped to establish me as one of the best heavyweight arm-wrestlers in the world. I now had a prestigious reputation, and I worked hard to maintain it over the next decade.

Another really good arm-wrestler I defeated was Richard Lupkes, considered by some to be the best in the world for a while. Richard Lupkes was a farmer from Minnesota, a massive 300-pound man with tree-trunk arms. Against Lupkes, I won the first match but lost the next two. My problem was that I let him beat me — I let his size and his reputation intimidate me. Despite his imposing looks, Lupkes is actually a very kind and gracious person. But he looks awesome at the table, and that can be hard to deal with. Lupkes was the top dog for a while, but he ended up getting into pro wrestling and injuring his shoulder, ruining his arm-wrestling career.

Johnny "Iceman" Walker was another legend in the sport of arm-wrestling I defeated. He was a professional arm-wrestler in the truest sense of the term, having spent a lifetime competing, training, observing, and testing out what techniques worked the best. Walker had so much experience that he could detect the strengths and weaknesses of an opponent even before the match began. Just by looking at a guy, he knew right away how to attack and how to defend. Johnny was not a really big guy, probably less than 200 pounds, but he had these monster hands, a huge wrist, and thick, long fingers like steel hooks. Because of that, I always attacked Johnny's whole arm, which was the only way I could even hope to beat him.

· · ·

In my mid-20s, I worked for a bit as a construction worker for the same family that had employed me as a bouncer. I've hardly ever been fired from a job in my life, but I didn't have the construction job for very long. I was working on a building in Barrie called Bayshore Landing, and I was getting paid $25 an hour, which was pretty good money for someone that young. At the site, two superintendents, George and Nick, controlled everything. George and I got along very well. Nick, on the other hand, was an idiot. I didn't like him from the get-go, and he probably didn't like me even before that. He was an asshole, and it was only a matter of time before things blew up between us.

One day I was cleaning up around the worksite, when George came up to me and said, "Gary, I want you to go upstairs and clean the floors. Sweep everything into the dumpster down on the second floor."

"What about the tarps?" I asked.

"We've got lots of tarps," he said. "If there are any ripped-up tarps, throw them out. If there are any good ones, keep them."

I went up to the third floor and started sweeping, like I was told to do. Sweeping was a dirty job, and I had to wear a face mask to prevent me from choking. Halfway through the job I was completely white and could hardly breathe, even with the mask on. All of a sudden I could hear Nick from the level below, screaming, "Gary, what the hell are you doing?! Are you stupid? What is wrong with you?" At first I was confused and started looking around, thinking that Nick must be talking to another Gary. I walked over to the ledge and looked down to see what was going on. By that point, everybody on the site could hear Nick's booming voice.

"Are you stupid, Gary? You're throwing away good tarps!"

Right away I got hot, and my blood started boiling. Here I was doing what I had been told to do, and Nick was belittling me in front of everybody. I've never taken humiliation well, and once I get challenged, I meet the challenge. I was furious and screamed back down, "What?! You piece of shit. I'm gonna come down there, rip your fucking head off, and shove it up your ass."

As soon as I said those words, I knew my job was gone. There was no point in trying to make it any better so I thought I might as well keep going. I took one step back and jumped into the garbage bin a floor below. The bin was filled with bricks, mortar, blocks of cement, steel bars, and nails and I could've easily landed on any of it; however, at that point I just didn't care — I jumped in without even thinking about it. I jumped in and out of the garbage bin in one fluid motion, ending up right in front of Nick's face. I was screaming so hard, and my saliva was hitting him. "I'm gonna shove your head up your ass," I yelled. "You say one word out of line with me right now and you're going to the hospital." Just like I had done with my former vice-principal, I was daring Nick to do anything. "Push me, touch me, say the wrong thing right now, and your life is done," I warned him.

At only 5'8" and 160 pounds, Nick was not a big guy. As soon as I landed in front of him, he shut up. He stayed really quiet, clearly realizing he'd pushed me too far. By the time I was finished screaming, everybody at the construction site was looking at us. I started settling down because when I knew Nick had been physically intimidated and verbally beat down, I started calming down and pulling back right away. Nick started barking at me again. "Are you done? Are you done?" he asked.

"Yeah," I said. "I'm done now."

"Well, when you settle down," he said, "come see me in my office."

With that, Nick turned around, took about three steps away, and then flicked the end of his cigarette at me. It whizzed by my face. Looking back, I'm glad the cigarette didn't hit me, because if it had, I would have gone crazy on Nick. After he left, everybody on the site came over to congratulate me. Nobody liked Nick. He was an arrogant prick to everybody, and I earned the respect of my coworkers by standing up to him. I didn't really give a shit about their respect though: I wasn't there for anybody else. I was only there to make money.

About an hour after the confrontation, I went to the construction site office to speak with Nick and clear some things up. When I got there I could hear him yelling into the phone: "I want him outta here. He's gone! I don't care. Pay him until the end of the week if you have to. I don't care." He finally spotted me and hung up the phone. "Gary," he said. "I want you gone today. You'll be paid until the end of next week and then you're done." I knew there was no point in protesting, so I just nodded my head and walked to the parking lot.

That very same day, I walked into the Honda auto plant in Alliston, Ontario, and got hired as a welder. Honda was a "dead job," meaning that it paid well but you never had to think. People old enough to remember the television show *Laverne & Shirley* will remember seeing them working at a bottling plant and putting their gloves on the bottles as they passed by. Working at Honda was just as boring. All you do is watch things go by every second of every minute of every day. People try and make it sound good, but the truth is that working in a factory is just a dead man's job. But it paid decent money and a lot of my friends worked there, which made it bearable.

. . .

In 1990, not too long after I started working at Honda, I entered a huge arm-wrestling tournament in Houston, Texas. I was defending the world championship titles that I had won over the previous four years. After tearing through the field and beating American John Smith in the finals to win the tournament, I met a man who invited me to compete at an upcoming tournament at the Super Bras de Fer in Paris, France. There was a lot of money involved, and all of the best arm-wrestlers in the world would be there. Needless to say, I didn't say no.

At the Brassie before the competition, everybody backstage was stretching and getting ready to compete when I saw the best-looking woman I'd ever seen in my life. This lady was a total doll, with curly black hair, beautiful brown eyes, and a smile to die for. It was love at first sight. She was so striking, I had to go tell her that she was a gorgeous human being. Her name was Katherine, and she was an arm-wrestler and doctor from England. Katherine told me we had met before at the arm-wrestling tournament in Houston. Hearing that really surprised me, because I didn't recall meeting her, and I *guarantee* I would have remembered that face.

The women in my life always seem to overlap, meaning that when I finish dating one woman, there's always another girlfriend ready to step in. When Katherine and I met, I had been living for a year and a half with a woman named Maggie, who was 14 years older than me. However, as soon as I got to know Katherine, I knew I had to break up with Maggie. Katherine told me she wanted to come to Canada to visit me, which to me meant I had to buy a house. I mean you can't be living in somebody's basement when you're dating a doctor. Katherine and I had a great time during her visit, and we dated for about a year and a half. Mostly we would talk on the phone, visiting each other once in a while. Spending hours talking on the phone meant that our relationship was pretty expensive, so eventually, since neither one of us wanted to move, the relationship just kind of fizzled out.

One night, a few years after we had stopped dating, I got a call informing me that Katherine had died. Katherine was anorexic, but when I met her she had her condition under control, and she looked great because she had put on a bunch of weight. She must've fallen back into anorexic behavior not too long after we stopped dating. Katherine died trying to get out of the bathtub at her home; in her weakened state, she fell and hit her head on the faucet, knocking her out. She didn't drown, because her nose stayed above the water, but she was unconscious and she eventually died of hypothermia. The news of Katherine's death devastated me. At the same time, I was grateful that I had the chance to know such a wonderful human being.

CHAPTER FOUR

A lot of people want to know the state of mind that leads a man to become a fighter. They want to know the background, because a prostitute is never born a prostitute — she had to get there somehow. It's the same with fighters. There's always a story behind the fighter.

Growing up, as far as I was concerned, my dad and I were best friends. We were like Pete and Repeat. My dad could tell me, "Gary, go jump out that window," and I would do it, because I loved my dad. Since I loved my father, I used to tell him everything. We were so close that when I reached my teens, I even told him about my sexual encounters. I remember after my first threesome I called my dad to tell him. I just had to get it off my chest, and there was nobody else I was close enough with to tell.

It wasn't until I was about 21 years old that I discovered my dad was using the stories I told him for his own sexual perversions. As a kid I really cherished the relationship I had with my father. However, looking back on it now as a grown man, I see exactly what my dad was doing and where he got the fuel for his fire. Some of his fuel came from me and the things that we used to talk about together. I see now how ridiculous it was. How can a son openly talk to his father about masturbation and having a threesome? They shouldn't, because it's not normal. There are certain boundaries that should be sacred between a father and his children.

Much worse than having inappropriate conversations with me, my dad was also abusive with the women in his life. Growing up, I never recognized any of the signs; I only found out what had happened when I was 21 years old and already out of the house. When everything came out, I sat down and talked to my sisters about some of the things they had been through. It was like we had never even lived in the same country, let alone the same house. My sisters lived in fear every day of their lives because all they ever knew was abuse.

The abuse my father inflicted is such a touchy subject within my family; we don't ever talk about it. We all just assume it is known. I actually don't even know if my entire family is comfortable with me sharing this part of our family history. However, if they are not comfortable right now, they will be in time. Change is what this world is all about.

Finding out the truth about my father affected me a great deal. I had loved the man I thought my father was. After the truth came out, the illusion was shattered and everything just broke down from there.

I never talk to my father now, and I don't accept anything from him. I know that he got remarried years ago and has three or four other new kids. I hope for their sake that my father has changed. The abuse that my dad inflicted on our family is one of several obstacles that have made me into a fighter. After everything I've been through personally, I can deal with anything my opponent wants to try and hurt me with in a fight.

The fight game is give and take, and sometimes you've got to take. A lot of guys can dish out punishment, but they can't take it. You've got to be able to take it too. I can give and take. I can punch the shit out of guys, but I can also get hit. Sometimes it's not my day and someone knocks the piss out of me — but I stick around. As long as my arm or neck isn't being broken, I won't tap out. People have said to me, "Gary, you took several knees to the head. Why didn't you stop?"

What would I stop for? There's still a chance for me to win the fight, because I know that, at any given point in a 15 to 30 minute fight, I can beat anybody if I hit him in the right place at the right time. It's all about mental toughness, which is something I've developed as a result of all of the experiences in my life.

· · ·

I continued to compete in arm-wrestling for quite a long time because I was good at it. Winning felt good, so it was hard to stop. But I also knew that I could never make a career out of it. There just wasn't enough money in it. I had been arm-wrestling competitively since the age of 15, and although I loved the sport, I was looking to make my mark somewhere else.

I had always felt that I had a lot to offer the world as a boxer. I mean, what guy wouldn't want to make a bunch of money by kicking some ass and knocking people out? There were other reasons I thought boxing was what I wanted to do. First of all, you get respect from people who don't even know you. Secondly, not only do you get the respect, you get the women.

I knew I wanted to be a boxer, but I didn't know how to box. Since Barrie isn't exactly the Mecca of the boxing world, I didn't even know where to train or where to look for help. Fortunately, I met someone by chance who knew exactly what it would take to mold me into the champion I wanted to be. I was walking through a department store in Barrie, talking with one of my friends about boxing, when suddenly this stranger turned around and said, "Hey, you're Gary Goodridge, aren't you? You're that arm-wrestler!"

"Yeah," I said. "I'm a pretty good arm-wrestler."

"No, no, no," he said. "You're not *pretty good*. You're the world champion!"

This guy and I got to talking about arm-wrestling, and eventually I told him that I thought I had something to offer the world of boxing. As it turned out, he was Norm Bell, a retired boxer who had just started training other people. Next thing I knew, Norm and I were exchanging numbers and making an appointment to train together. I couldn't believe it — it seemed like fate to have randomly met a boxing coach in the middle of a department store.

Norm soon started training me. I had never done any kind of boxing before; Norm had to break it down from scratch for me. First, he taught me how to throw a jab. Next, he taught me how to throw a cross, a hook, and an uppercut. Once I had the basics down, Norm taught me the most important part of boxing, which is putting combinations together. It took a little bit of adjusting to go from arm-wrestling to boxing, since there is a major difference in the type of strength training for each sport. In arm-wrestling, you're not supposed to move, and you need to be tight and rigid. Boxing is just the opposite — you've got to be loose, and you've got to be able to extend your arm, which was always difficult for me. To this day, I still can't fully extend my right arm — arm-wrestling had shortened the tendons and pulled everything together with scar tissue.

I didn't have the money to train at a fancy gym, so Norm and I would train wherever we could find space. Sometimes we'd train in my backyard or my garage. Other times we'd go out to a farm Norm had access to and we'd train in the chicken coop or scratch out a little spot in the pig barn. We never had a real place to train, so we always trained in the nastiest, most horrendous locations. It was just like in *Rocky,* with Norm as Mickey, the rough but brilliant trainer.

From the moment we met, I was Norm's pride and joy. He had such a passion for boxing, and since he was no longer competing, I provided him with a link to the sport. When I went running, Norm would ride his bike beside me, talking to me every step of the way. Most of the time I could barely breathe or speak, but Norm would be right beside me the whole time, telling me what to do. Norm would always say things like, "Come on, pick it up, Gary. Let's go," then he'd ride a little faster on his bike, forcing me to catch up.

Norm quickly realized that I was going to need sparring partners if I was going to eventually compete. Since there was nobody around with my size and ability, I had to drive over an hour to Toronto to find suitable partners. Norm would insist on being there every time to watch and analyze my sparring sessions. On the ride home, we'd always go over what had happened, and Norm would point out all of the different things I needed to work on. All of the hard work eventually paid off, because it wasn't long before I started getting real fights and knocking guys out.

Three months after I started training with Norm, I won my first amateur bout against a boxer named Jesse T. Hill, in Akron, Ohio. A few months later, I beat Brad Evaschuk at the Atlas Amateur Boxing Club. My third fight, in London, Ontario, was against Wayne Moe, and earned me the super heavyweight championship of Ontario. Following that, I defended my provincial title against top local boxers Chris Babes, Richard Hall, and Peter Bottello Shamrock.

Ten months from the day Norm helped me into my first pair of boxing gloves, I became the Canadian Amateur Super Heavyweight Boxing Champion. In order to fight for the championship, fighters were supposed to have had at least 10 amateur fights. When I challenged for the belt, I had only fought six times, one of which was an exhibition match. I wasn't even supposed to be in the championship, because I was green as hell and I probably could have easily gotten hurt. The reason that I was rushed into a title fight was because all of the top amateur boxers who had competed in the 1992 summer Olympics the previous year in Barcelona had gone on to become professionals. That made 1993 a year of beginners in the Canadian amateur boxing scene, and I just happened to be the best of the beginners.

To win the super heavyweight boxing title, I beat a tough character from Nova Scotia named Scott McClung. Since the fight took place in his hometown, I went into that bout as enemy number one. At the start of the fight, I came out and just started swinging. I wanted to beat my opponent as fast as I could, because I didn't want to stick around and get beaten with punches for too long. I was smart enough to know that I didn't have the experience to get into a drawn-out tactical battle. In the end, my plan to bum-rush my opponent worked, because I knocked him down three times early in the first round. After the third knockdown, the referee called the fight so McClung wouldn't get seriously hurt.

The reason that I won the championship that year, other than good timing, was because I was more determined than anybody else. I definitely didn't win because of my technique, since I was still throwing punches from my waist — anyone who knows anything about boxing knows you can't do that. You have to throw punches properly or you're going to end up on your ass. Luckily, I hit hard enough that when I forced my opponent into an all-out brawl, he just couldn't take the pressure.

My family and friends had no idea exactly how big of an accomplishment winning the championship was. Norm Bell was probably happier than anybody else, because he knew its significance. I was also very happy, because I had finally found something other than arm-wrestling that I was actually good at. It seemed like things were starting to fall into place. I went into arm-wrestling as a peon and went on to become a nine-time world champion. With boxing, I was able to go from being a peon to a champion again. I knew what it was like to taste victory, and it only made me want it more.

Victory would have to come from somewhere other than the boxing ring, however, because my career as a pugilist didn't last very long. After I became the Canadian Amateur Super Heavyweight Boxing Champion, I had my first international boxing fight against a fighter from San Bernardino, California, named David "The Boss" Bostice. The fight took place in Florida and was billed as the best in Canada versus the best in the United States. Boxers from the U.S. are traditionally seen as better because of the large size of their pool of competitors and the quality of their amateur program. Our fight definitely didn't do anything to dispel the notion that U.S. boxers are superior to Canadians.

By the time I fought David Bostice, I weighed a relatively gaunt 213 pounds. I had been over 250 pounds when I began my boxing training rounds, but working at Honda and doing intense workouts with Norm Bell just sucked the weight right off me, even without dieting. David Bostice, who later went on to box professionally against notables like Wladimir Klitschko and Jeremy Williams, was younger, more experienced, and just an all-around better boxer than me. Despite his advantages, I came to fight that day, and we ended up having a three-round war. In the first round I was beating up Bostice by bringing the fight to him and keeping the pressure on. As it turned out, I should have paced myself better, because I ended up gassing myself out in the first round. The second round was somewhat even, but by the third round, Bostice just mopped up the floor with me. Since there was nothing left in my gas tank, I couldn't stage any kind of offense in the last half of the fight. Without offense, I just ended up becoming a punching bag for Bostice. He hit me so many times in the final round that my kids are probably still dizzy from it today. Mercifully, the referee ended up stopping the fight 15 minutes before the end, giving Bostice the win.

Norm Bell hadn't been able to come with me to Florida, but he had asked me to call him after the fight to tell him the result. After the fight, I couldn't remember where I was or what I was doing. It was the first time that I had ever experienced any kind of brain damage from a fight, in terms of memory loss. I knew my name, but that was about it. I knew that I had to call Norm but I couldn't remember why. When I called him on the phone, I said, "Yeah, Norm, I remembered that I was supposed to call you, but I can't remember what I was calling you for." Norm knew right away that I wasn't firing on all cylinders. He asked me if I'd seen the doctor, and I told him that the ring doctor had checked me out. Norm knew I needed real medical attention, and that I wasn't in the right state of mind to get help for myself. He made me put somebody else on the phone and told them I needed to see a doctor, which I did.

As it turned out, I had suffered a pretty severe concussion. David

Bostice had beaten me like a punching bag for the entire third round, and it showed on my face. Back in the hotel room, I looked in the mirror at my badly bruised and swollen face and decided that I was allergic to boxing. I needed to choose another career. The sport of boxing is just shots to the head over and over again. Sure, there's the odd shot to the stomach, but that's only to get your hands down for another hit to the head. Boxing is just head trauma, and I didn't want to subject myself to that. I love myself too much to get in a ring and let somebody bounce my brains around. Because up until then, I had been the one who was beating other people. It took me a while to realize that fact. As soon as I got my butt kicked, however, I knew boxing wasn't for me.

Another reason boxing wasn't working out for me was that it demands total commitment, to the exclusion of everything else. Boxing improves overall coordination, timing, explosiveness, and determination, and is very much the opposite of arm-wrestling. It relies on outward movements and extensions, whereas arm-wrestling is basically an inward movement, a flexing of the muscles rather than an extension. Boxing uses jabbing and other movements similar to throwing a baseball or a football; those types of movements would likely cause an arm-wrestler to hyperextend his arm. A boxer wants to keep his muscles relaxed and flexible, while arm-wrestling requires that all your muscles be tense and loaded like a spring ready to release. I simply couldn't do both, and so I went back to the sport I was best at.

• • •

In the mid-1990s, I was at the peak of my arm-wrestling ability, and there weren't many people in the world that stood a chance at beating me. One arm-wrestler who did beat me was John Brzenk, a puller against whom I'd had many epic grapples. I first met John at the Over-the-Top Championship when he won the open weight division. Pound-for-pound, Brzenk is probably the best arm-wrestler who has ever lived. When you're talking about arm-wrestling, you have to talk about Brzenk. Even *The Guinness Book of World Records* named him the best arm-wrestler in the world because he had beaten most of the top heavyweights. Despite his success against heavyweights, Brzenk's not even a huge guy. He only weighs about 210 pounds; however, he's got an incredibly strong right arm and great technique. From 1987 to 1996, John and I faced each other dozens of times. In most competitions we would both usually go through the rest of the field and then end up against each other in the finals. It always came down to John and me; sometimes I'd win, and sometimes he'd win.

In August 1995, I traveled to New York City to compete at the Yukon Jack Arm-wrestling Championships. In previous years, the Yukon Jack Championships had featured the top pullers in North America only. In 1995, they decided to expand their championship by inviting the best arm-wrestlers from all over the world, including Brazil, England, Sweden, and other countries known for having the top grapplers. It was a great opportunity to showcase my skills, but I knew that I had my work cut out for me. With 2,500 people attending the event, and tens of thousands more watching the ESPN broadcast at home, the pressure was on to perform on the big stage.

Thankfully, the one person I didn't have to worry about this time was John Brzenk. Before the competition, Brzenk had decided to cut some weight and drop down to the 198-pound weight class. Even though there was no doubt that John Brzenk could grapple with the best heavyweights in the world, it was probably the right choice, because the field that day was huge. Besides myself at 260 pounds, there was also the 300-pound Georgian giant Zaur Tskhadadze and Cleve Dean, a 450-pound pig farmer. In the first three out of five rounds, I quickly disposed of all of my opponents, Johan Siswantoro, David Randall, and Jerry Cadorette.

Then I faced off against Cleve Dean. Cleve was an absolute legend in the arm-wrestling world, having been the undisputed heavyweight champion from the late 1970s to the mid-'80s. Cleve and I first met in 1986 at the Over-the-Top Championship in Las Vegas. Cleve Dean won the heavyweight division and was supposed to play Sylvester Stallone's final opponent in the movie. But at the last minute, the producers decided Cleve was too big and that it would look unrealistic if Sly's character beat him. In the end, Rick Zumwalt ended up getting the part.

Shortly after Over-the-Top, Cleve had some personal problems, retired from the sport of arm-wrestling, and ballooned to over 700 pounds. However, that wasn't the last of him. In 1994, at the age of 40, Cleve lost the extra weight and returned to the world of arm-wrestling at the Yukon Jack in San Francisco. That year, Cleve became the world champion again after defeating me in epic matches that left us both injured and bruised. I hate losing, so after the loss I trained hard on the weights and tables and really dedicated myself to becoming the best arm-wrestler in the world. Even though Cleve Dean was a behemoth and a legend, I knew that I was capable of beating him. In New York City, I got the chance to prove it to the rest of the world.

Going into the match against Cleve, I was the underdog, not only because I had lost to him the previous year, but also because he's so big. Cleve's got enormous hands, like a baseball catcher's glove. Next to him, I looked like a three-year-old wrestling a full-grown man. Cleve's hand engulfed everything, and you couldn't even see my hand when he closed up on me. He was so powerful; he usually completely controlled his opponents. But I had a good strategy: I decided to try an arm-wrestling maneuver called the top-roll on him. In a top-roll, you hold onto the thumb of your opponent, not the fingers like the classic arm-wrestling style. Then you pull your arm toward your shoulder and try and peel your opponent's hand off the back of yours, going against their finger as opposed to their arm. If you have a big hand, you can top-roll easily, which is how Cleve Dean usually won. If you've got a smaller hand like me, then you have to go inside. The problem with trying to do that against Cleve was, up until that point, nobody had ever top-rolled him. That didn't deter me. I just went for it in the semi-finals and ended up pinning Cleve and getting the win.

Going into the fifth and final round at the 1995 Yukon Jack, I was undefeated but I still had to beat Cleve again in order to take home first place, since it was a double elimination tournament and Cleve had only lost to me. On our final pull I could tell that Cleve was going for a top-roll, so I took my fingers off the back of his hand and slipped out. Slipping out of our grip on purpose meant Cleve and I would have to use the strap. Once you're in the straps, you can't maneuver, which means that size doesn't matter — it's all about who is stronger. Once the strap was in place, I could tell that Cleve was tired. As soon as we started, I flashed him really quick, pinning his hand for the win. At first, there was dead silence, then I jumped up shouting, and the crowd roared with approval.

After I beat Cleve Dean and the rest of the Yukon Jack heavyweight class, John Brzenk and I decided to grapple for fun to entertain the crowd. Brzenk had won the middleweight championship and wanted to have a go at me again since I had beaten him in the 1994 Yukon Jack. Nothing was different in 1995, and I ended up beating Brzenk four out of five times. It was a great finish to a great day in my arm-wrestling career. In the course of one day, I had decisively beaten two of my biggest rivals.

When I started arm-wrestling, I could always reach deep and get more strength to pull off a win if I needed to. A lot of people used to tell me they'd never seen anything like it in their lives. Sometimes we'd be training for arm-wrestling and I would get frustrated that I was getting beat. All of a sudden, I'd decide that was the last time I was getting beat that day, and I would not go down after that. That's the kind of inner power and mind control I had back then. That's why I dominated arm-wrestling for 11 years, even though my hand was so small. Guys like Cleve Dean had hands twice the size of mine and were stronger, but I would still beat them. There were times when nobody could beat my heart or my mind control. One of my biggest strengths was that I was incredibly fast — nobody had a faster start in competitions than me, and it really worked to my advantage. I always wanted to be bigger, faster, and better.

At 29 years old, I was a nine-time world champion heavyweight arm-wrestler, but I was starting to lose the passion I once had for the sport. I was looking to make my mark someplace else; I just didn't know where yet. Little did I know, an opportunity was coming around the corner that would cement my reputation as a tough guy and change my life forever.

CHAPTER FIVE

After winning the 1995 Yukon Jack arm-wrestling championship, I floated around for a while, trying to find out exactly what I wanted to do with my life. One day, some buddies of mine came over to my house and brought a tape of Ultimate Fighting Championship 2 with them. I had never seen the UFC before, but I had heard crazy stories about brutal fights in which people would break multiple bones and keep on fighting. I couldn't understand why anyone would want to do something like that. When I actually sat down and watched UFC, however, I loved the sport right away. I was amazed when I saw Remco Pardoel elbow the hell out of Orlando Weit's head. I was in awe at how Remco was able to almost crush another man's skull with devastating elbow shots. My friends started trying to convince me to fight in the UFC. Of course, I was with the guys and needed to show some bravado, so I said, "Yeah, I can do that. It looks easy." Even as I was saying it I was just killing myself inside, thinking there was *no way* I wanted any part of that kind of violence.

The next thing I knew, a phone number plugging UFC merchandise popped up on the screen. Right away my friends got the idea to call the number. Surprisingly, somebody picked up the other line. "We don't want to buy anything," one of my friends said. "We've got somebody here who can fight!" In no time, my friends had UFC co-creator and matchmaker Art Davie on the phone, and they were telling him they had somebody who could kick ass in the UFC. I was scared as hell at the thought of cagefighting, but at that point, I couldn't say no. I had to step up because I was in a room with four or five guys who were all pumped up and trying to encourage me.

Art is only 5'4", but on the phone that night he sounded like he was eight feet tall and 400 pounds, and I quickly realized that Art was shrewd and very good at what he does. He got to the point right away and asked me what kind of experience I had. I told him I had been doing martial arts since I was 10 years old, which was a bunch of crap. Sure, I had taken a couple of martial arts classes as a kid, but I hadn't lasted long. In fact, I'd hated those classes. It was just a bunch of katas, which was like practicing choreographed dance moves. You never actually got to hit anybody.

In the midst of talking myself up, Art suddenly recognized my name. "Gary Goodridge?!" he shouted. "I just watched you beat that behemoth in arm-wrestling the other day." As it turned out, Art had seen me beat Cleve Dean on ESPN. He was a big fan of Cleve's and had watched Cleve dominate strength sports, like lifting kegs and pulling trains. Since Art Davie had just seen me defeat this seemingly unbeatable giant, he figured it had to be fate that I was calling him. "We absolutely have a spot for you in the UFC," he said. "You spoke really well on television, and the UFC needs more people like you."

The next day Art called to tell me I would be a part of UFC 8: David vs Goliath. At this point, I didn't consider myself very big, so I had to ask, "Well, which am I? A David or a Goliath?" Art told me I was going to be the smallest Goliath and that my opponent, Paul Herrera, would be the smallest David at 185 pounds. Art told me Herrera was a University of Nebraska all-American wrestler and a two-time judo champion. Even better, he called himself a street fighter and was David "Tank" Abbott's protégé. At the time, Tank Abbot was knocking the piss out of people in the UFC left, right, and center. I couldn't help but think that Tank's top dog would knock the piss out of me.

I had no idea what I was doing. The fight was in one month and 12 days. Even though I had been an amateur boxing champion, I really didn't know anything about fighting. I was one hundred percent green. Hell, I was still punching from my hip. I was just a tough guy. I had no idea that you needed cardio to fight. People ask me, "How could you not know you had to be in shape?" Well, I just didn't know. I trained with people who didn't know anything about martial arts either, so they weren't able to give me anything. I was just a big kid who was looking to find himself.

I needed to try and find somebody to train with who knew more than I did. When I took on my first UFC fight, I was still working at the Honda factory. A good friend of mine who worked there was a guy named Phong Tran, and he offered to help me prepare for the fight. Phong was a small but muscular guy. He was super nice, but he really didn't know anything about fighting. The martial arts he did were just for show. He did things like acrobatic flying kicks and weapons training, which made him look like a Teenage Mutant Ninja Turtle. He looked amazing doing it, but it wasn't practical. Nevertheless, Phong was a big asset to me at the time, because he was one of the only people I had who I could train with.

I knew that everybody in the UFC had credentials and I had nothing, so Phong and I started looking for a gym that would give me a certificate. We ended up finding a gym that taught Kuk Sool Won, a Korean martial art focused on striking, joint locks, and chokes. The guy who ran the place was named Mr. Lee. When I told him I was going to fight in the UFC, Mr. Lee said, "I've got another guy here named John who wants to fight in the UFC too. He's not here today, but if you come in here another day, I'll have you two fight each other. Whoever wins can represent the school." That sounded fine to me. Taking a look around, I saw there was a little peanut butter jar on the front counter that had some change in it. On it was a label that read "Help John make it to the UFC." I guess John didn't have very much support, because the jar only had about five dollars in it.

One day while I was training at Mr. Lee's, John came in. We ended up chatting for a while, and John turned out to be a really nice guy. He was muscular but only weighed about 160 pounds. On the other hand, I was 260 pounds and filled with the right stuff. John and I decided we wouldn't actually fight. Instead, we'd just see who won a grappling contest. As soon as John and I started wrestling, I quickly got on top and stayed there. John knew a lot of techniques but couldn't use any of them and got frustrated because I was just too large for him. After a few minutes of grappling, it was obvious I was the better fighter. Not only could I easily hold John down, I also had boxing experience and could hit hard. When the match was done, I turned to Mr. Lee and asked jokingly, "So does the jar come home with me?"

I trained in Kuk Sool Won for the few weeks leading up to the UFC fight. I wanted written credentials just in case the UFC asked for them, and Mr. Lee told me that in order to get them, I would have to represent his club by wearing his gi during the fight. Since I needed the certificate, I agreed. I thought that if Royce Gracie could win in the UFC while wearing a gi, why couldn't I? Less than a month after I entered Mr. Lee's gym, I became a certified fourth-degree black belt in Kuk Sool Won. I was really happy about getting it at the time, and I'm still really proud of it to this day. I only used Kuk Sool Won to describe my style of fighting for the first year of my fighting career, but even today some people still run with it. People don't like to say how I got my black belt, but I have no problem telling the truth: it was given to me.

Even though I had outwrestled John at Mr. Lee's gym, I knew that I had only won because of pure strength. If I was going to stand a chance against UFC-caliber fighters, I had to learn actual grappling techniques. I watched the early UFC videos to study the type of submissions Royce Gracie was doing. Before he came along, nobody knew anything about submissions. To most people it was just Brazilian nonsense. However, the truth was that if you wanted to be able to beat guys who knew submissions, you had to learn Brazilian Jiu-jitsu. Ever since I started in mixed martial arts, I've been learning how to do arm bars, especially from the top, and a variety of other techniques. I've learned that submissions can be great and can work all the time when practicing; however, they can also get you into a lot of trouble in actual fights if you aren't able to finish the submission.

I also watched a lot of Dan "The Beast" Severn's fights; at the time, he was beating everybody in the UFC with his wrestling skills. Dan Severn had won many international wrestling awards and had spent some time as a professional wrestler before entering mixed martial arts at UFC 4. After Royce Gracie dominated the first couple of UFCs, fighters started learning submission defense, and wrestlers like Dan Severn became serious contenders. I recognized this and knew I would need to work on my wrestling skills in order to have any sort of success. Back in the day, Severn was a good fighter for the same reason Royce Gracie had been: because nobody knew what they were doing. Severn was good, but people nowadays understand how to beat pure wrestlers.

I decided that in order to save myself from a wrestler like Dan Severn, I needed to find a wrestler to train with. Through word of mouth, I found John Gnap, who lived about half an hour outside of Barrie. People were telling me to train with this guy because he knew everything about wrestling. After hearing so much about him, I called John up one day and asked him if we could train together. John told me, "I don't want to train with you if you can't beat me. So come on over. If you can beat me, you can train with me. If not, I've got to look you over." It was plain and simple like that.

When we finally got together, I was very impressed with his skills. John was smaller and 10 years older than me, but he was cut from granite. He was an amazing freestyle wrestler and had been part of the Hungarian national squad that competed in the 1976 Montreal Olympics. John also tried out for the Canadian Olympic team years later and nearly made it. The entire goal of my first training session with John Gnap was to try and dominate him on the ground. Whenever I would try to take him down, John would have to crush it, hold me down, and then we'd start again. We wrestled back and forth for quite a while, and at the end of it, John was impressed with me and agreed to help train me.

Even though he is a really tough guy, John Gnap is also the happiest person you'll ever meet. He's always "almost wonderful." Even if the whole world was falling down around him, John would still have a smile on his face. When we'd go on fight trips, everyone used to joke that we'd be "John'd out" because he was so damn happy. I'm so glad I met him, and I truly believe he was essential to the success that I've had in mixed martial arts.

I knew that I needed some corner men, so I asked my cousin Garvin Lewis, Phong Tran, Phil Stoppart, John Gnap, and Mike Mobbs to accompany me. I dubbed Mike Mobbs my manager, but he wasn't a manager in the traditional sense. Instead, Mike was there to be my eyes when I couldn't see. I had no idea what was going to happen when I fought in the cage. It was entirely possible that I could get knocked out and would need somebody there whom I trusted to make the best decisions for me. Mike Mobbs was the man for the job, without a doubt.

Along with having corner men, I also knew that every fighter had to have a nickname, so I started telling all of my friends to suggest a nickname. A friend of mine came up with "Big Pimp Daddy." Earlier that day I had been reading about a football player called "Big Daddy." I thought that was a cool nickname, so I dropped the "pimp" and decided to go with "Big Daddy." Despite the fact that my friends were all very supportive and excited, I was afraid to tell anybody in my family that I was fighting, so I didn't. The last thing I wanted to do was lose the fight with my whole family watching.

When I finally arrived in Bayamon, Puerto Rico, for UFC 8, it was over a hundred degrees. There were a lot of problems with the UFC putting on an event in Puerto Rico. The government held a lot of the equipment up at the border because they didn't want the UFC in their country. That meant that the organization had a training room set up in the hotel, but there were no mats. In Bayamon the atmosphere was electric because of the UFC show. It was hard not to get swept up in all of the hype. I'd been to all kinds of arm-wrestling tournaments, and I'd done some boxing, so I had an idea of what I was getting myself into, but I really wasn't prepared for the magnitude of the UFC. I tried to play it low-key, because I knew that fighting one of Tank's guys was serious business. I was there to fight, not to mess around.

In the lead-up to the fight, some of my friends told me that Tank Abbott was a racist skinhead who was involved with the Klu Klux Klan. Of course it wasn't true, but my friends said it so I would train harder and have more aggression going into the fight against Tank's protégé Paul Herrera. It's what my team thought I needed. It turned out to be a good idea, because I ended up coming out for the first fight extremely aggressive and looking for blood. Going into the Herrera fight, I wasn't confident at all in my technical fighting abilities; however, I was confident that I wasn't going to lose to this guy. I swore up and down that I was not going to lose to this racist jerk. I didn't care what I needed to do because, in my mind, I was now fighting for all black people.

In order to try and develop a strategy for my fight, the guys in my corner decided to shadow Paul Herrera for the weekend to see what he was doing. At one point we all went down to the beach where there was a stage set up to film the fighter introductions for the pay per view production. The UFC had scheduled a time for each fighter to show up to demonstrate his style for the cameras. When it was my time, I didn't know what to do, so I just started punching. I looked into the camera and said, "There are three things that I'm bringing into this UFC that nobody's ever brought in all together at once before: superior attitude, superior mind, superior strength. I've got it all, second to none. Big Daddy's bringing home the bacon."

After I was done my shtick, my friends stuck around to watch Herrera do his thing. One thing that really stuck out was that Herrera kept doing a wrestling move called the fireman's carry. He did a bunch of takes, and every time Herrera would shoot toward the camera, as if he was going to drop somebody over his shoulder with a double-leg takedown. As soon as they finished watching Herrera, my friends rushed up to my hotel room and told me that he was going to go for the fireman's carry. Armed with that information, my team and I stayed in my room until the wee hours of the morning trying to come up with a move to counter the fireman's carry.

The move we came up with was this: I would trap Herrera in the crucifix position, meaning I would take one of his arms in between my legs and then fall back while pulling his other arm down to the ground with me. With both of his arms isolated, I would be in a position to either break Herrera's arm or make him tap. We created some space in the hotel room by pushing the beds to the side and then practiced the crucifix move again and again for four straight hours. Phil Stoppart was roughly the same size as Herrera, so he was the guinea pig who had the move applied on him hundreds of times. We went over that move so many times, Phil got a carpet burn on his left elbow that lasted years. I practiced my counter move almost 1,000 times so that when I got out there to fight, it would be textbook. By the end of the night, I had beaten up everybody in my hotel room, and everybody was sore, including me.

The next night, when I got to Ruben Rodriguez Coliseum for the fight, the intensity backstage was extreme. Since there were no televisions in the back, nobody could see what was happening in the other fights. The only information about the fights we received was who was up next. Making matters worse, none of the fighters had their own dressing room. There were only little curtains separating each fighter, which meant that you could easily hear people warming up, farting, and doing whatever else they needed to do to get ready.

When my name was called to enter the Octagon, I had a lot of nervous energy and had to work hard to control myself. I was scared, because I wasn't sure if I was good enough or tough enough to compete in the UFC. Lots of people at work had been telling me that I was going to get my ass kicked against veteran fighters. Part of me couldn't help but think maybe they were right. The only thing that kept me optimistic was that fact that I wanted to win so badly. As far as I was concerned, Paul Herrera was a racist and there was absolutely no way I was going to let that asshole beat me up.

As soon as referee "Big" John McCarthy looked at us and barked his now-famous words — "Are you ready? Are you ready? Let's get it on!" — Herrera came across the Octagon at me. For a brief second, I just kind of waited to see if Herrera was going to do what I expected him to do. I had trained expecting Herrera to shoot on me, and that was exactly what he did. Had he come out and just started punching, it would've completely thrown me off but, for his first move, he faked a punch and then shot in to grab my right leg. As soon as he did, I sprawled on top of him and executed the exact move I had practiced hundreds of times the night before.

Once I got his arms trapped, my elbow went to work on his jaw and his temple. In all, I hit Herrera with eight elbows to the head. The first elbow knocked him out and made him go limp, and the rest happened so quickly it took Big John a few seconds to step in and stop the fight. I didn't know Herrera was knocked out, because I didn't feel anything — I was running on total adrenaline and energy. My arm was like a piston throwing the elbows. If Big John hadn't stepped in to stop the fight, I'd probably still be smashing in Herrera's face right now. The funny thing is, the plan was never to rifle Herrera in the head until he went to sleep. I was actually supposed to get him in the crucifix position and then apply a gooseneck submission to bend his wrist until he tapped. During the fight I just got too excited and started taking apart Herrera's head. Looking back, I'm glad I decided to go with the elbows because they led to one of the most memorable knockouts in UFC history. Unfortunately, it turned out that I ended up breaking Herrera's orbital bone and he needed to start wearing prescription glasses. But that's the risk we both took when we decided to step into the Octagon.

The feeling of winning was just an amazing out-of-body experience.

It was sort of like an orgasm: just unbelievable. I was so excited that in my celebration I ran into the top of the cage and almost knocked myself out. I had so much adrenaline pumping through my body before the fight that when I came down from the high after, it just drained me and I hit rock bottom really quickly.

I couldn't stay down for long, however. UFC 8 was set up as a tournament, and I had to get right back up again for the next fight. I had gone through Herrera like a hot knife through butter, but I knew my next fight, a semi-final match against Jerry Bohlander, wouldn't be as quick. Bohlander came out of the Lion's Den gym, where he trained with Ken Shamrock. That fact alone said a lot about Bohlander's toughness. Ken Shamrock was widely known among mixed martial arts fans. He had lost to Royce Gracie at UFC 1, but in the process, he had become a crowd favorite. Along with a draw against Royce Gracie at UFC 5 and a big win over wrestler Dan Severn by guillotine choke at UFC 6, Shamrock was also the first king of Pancrase, a respected Japanese shoot-fighting organization. Like facing Tank's protégé, a fight against Bohlander was a big deal because Shamrock was a rough customer, and back then, everybody wanted to be like him. In hindsight, Shamrock didn't know shit, but in 1996, knowing a little bit meant you knew a lot. These days the Lion's Den is for cubs, but back in the day it was a place where a lot of good guys trained together.

Jerry Bohlander was Ken Shamrock's top student on the Lion's Den team and his first student to get a shot fighting in the UFC. The Lion's Den mainly focused on submissions, which meant Bohlander had very decent ground skills, even by today's standards. Bohlander showcased his grappling skills in his first bout of the night at UFC 8 with his guillotine choke victory over the much bigger, 350-pound former college football player Scott Ferrozzo. Having heard backstage that Bohlander had just outwrestled a much larger opponent, I knew that in order to stand a chance at beating him, I was going to have to really use the wrestling techniques I had been working on with John Gnap. The game plan, which was put together quickly backstage, was to hold Bohlander down and keep his ankles by his head. That way I could deliver more punches and strikes to his head without having to worry about him thrusting me away with his legs.

When Big John started our semi-final fight, I stalked Bohlander and forced him into one of the corners. As soon as I threw a left hook, Bohlander shot in, but I was able to sprawl so he couldn't take me down. Bohlander kept going for the takedown, so I grabbed him around the neck and tried to put him in a guillotine choke and cut off the circulation to his head. However, when I picked him up and tried to slam him, Bohlander got out of the chokehold and we started clinching. After getting double underhooks on Bohlander, I went behind him, picked him up, and slammed us both to the mat. As soon as we hit the ground, I passed Bohlander's legs and ended up on top of him in side control. I held Bohlander in side control for a bit, in order to catch my breath, while he struggled to get out from under me. Every time I tried to posture up and unload on Bohlander, he would hold onto me, so I tried to smother him and wear him out on the ground. Finally, I swung my left leg over his body to mount him.

However, in the mount, I got a bit too high toward his chest and he was able to sweep me, ending up on top in my half-guard. I tried to hold him down, but he snuck his leg out from between mine, mounted me, and then hit me with a few punches and head butts. The shots didn't really hurt and mostly just glanced off me. Bohlander continued to hit me with some punches from the mount until I put everything I had into getting him off me. Posting my left arm on the mat, I rolled to my left, and when Bohlander tried to stop me from sweeping him, I turned toward the right and slammed him to the mat, ending up in his guard. I broke out of Bohlander's closed guard, postured up, and pushed him against the fence while pressing my left knee into his face. Bohlander tried to keep me at a distance and went for a leg lock, which I countered by trying to stomp on his face. At that point I realized that I had to increase the intensity, so I rained down some hard right hands.

Finally, Big John had seen enough damage and stepped in to stop the fight. It was a hundred times messier than the win over Herrera, but it was still a win.

Bohlander and I fought for over five minutes, and even though I had won, those five minutes just completely wore me out. Big John could tell that I was in a rough condition, so when the fight was over, he told me to go and get some rest. Outside of the Octagon, I had to rest for a minute on the stairs because I couldn't even hold myself up. As soon as I sat down, Mike Mobbs started yelling at me: "Gary, walk back. Walk upright. Carry yourself out. Don't let everybody see you like this!" I knew Mike was right, but I couldn't walk to the dressing room on my own. I just didn't have the energy. In my entire life I had never been that exhausted before. I had never even done anything remotely close to that. The roller coaster ride of fighting twice and coming down after two wins just left me so bloody tired. If you look at my second fight at UFC 8 you can see I was absolutely spent. I was holding onto the fence for support because I could barely stand. I won that fight with just pure determination and heart.

Since I was holding onto anything I could grab, my corner men put my arms around their shoulders and helped me stumble backstage. On the way, I was stopped for an interview by commentator and former Olympic gold medal wrestler Jeff Blatnick. "This is tough," I told Jeff, "tougher than I expected. All of these boys — I mean all of these men, pardon me — are very tough, and I'm just happy to be among them." When Blatnick asked if I thought I could win the whole tournament, it was hard to act confident, since I could barely stand on my own. "I certainly hope so" was my answer. "I'm going to do my best and continue what I've been doing. If somebody's better, then they'll beat me."

When I finally got backstage, I was absolutely done. I tried to tell my team that I couldn't fight anymore. Without the pressure of the camera forcing me to speak intelligently, only broken words came out through gasps of air. I could barely communicate how tired I was; there was definitely no way I was going to go into the cage just to be somebody's organic punching bag. Since I knew that the UFC had reserve fighters for the tournament in case someone got injured and couldn't compete, I told one of the UFC employees to let somebody else go on to the finals. I was done. A few minutes later Bob Meyrowitz, owner of the UFC, came up to me. He clearly wasn't happy. "So, you're done?" he asked.

"Yeah," I said. "I just don't have any energy."

Being the shrewd businessman that he is, Meyrowitz knew exactly what it would take to get me to fight in the finals. "Gary," he said, "if you get in the cage, you'll earn $10,000 tonight. If you don't fight, you'll only get the $2,500 I promised you'd get when you came here. It's a $7,500 call. Remember also, there's the chance that you could win the fight and walk away with $50,000 for winning the entire tournament. You make the decision. I'll be back in a minute."

Put like that, it was not a difficult decision to make, and when Bob Meyrowitz came back, I told him, "No problem, I'll do it." After accepting the fight, my corner and I turned our attention to Don Frye, my opponent in the finals. I knew going into the fight that Frye was a tough customer. Not only did he train at Arizona State with his coach and UFC legend Dan Severn, Frye was also an amateur boxer with lots of combat experience. In his first fight, Frye had faced San Juan's favorite hometown fighter, Thomas Ramirez. Ramirez, who was 410 pounds, had an infamous reputation, claiming to have won over 200 challenge matches on the island of Puerto Rico. Frye quickly silenced the hometown crowd, however, when he hit Ramirez on the chin with two quick punches, knocking him out in eight seconds, which stood as the quickest knockout in UFC history for many years. In the semi-finals, Frye again showed his prowess when he beat wrestler and amateur boxer Sam Adkins by TKO, due to a cut, only 48 seconds into the first round.

Since Frye's changing area was right beside mine, separated only by a small curtain, I knew he had probably heard my corner freaking out after the Bohlander fight, yelling things like, "Get him oxygen! Fan him! Take off his gi! He's too hot!" Meanwhile, Frye was bouncing around like he was full of energy after beating both of his opponents in less than one minute. In order to try and keep him from having a mental advantage, my corner and I started using only hand gestures and nods to communicate with each other so that Frye wouldn't be able to hear what we were strategizing about. Using that method, we decided the guys would start hitting the pads while I was still on the ground so that Frye would think that I was okay and warming up. We figured that way we could trick him into thinking I had recovered from my exhaustion really quickly.

Before the finals against Don Frye, a super fight took place between Ken Shamrock and Kimo Leopoldo. Shamrock won by a knee bar less than five minutes into the fight, which didn't give me very much time to recover. It felt like I had only just fought, but the next thing I knew, Frye and I were in the Octagon for the main event of the evening. We were the last two warriors. He was the biggest David, I was the smallest Goliath, and we were going to war. By the time I got into the cage, I had regained some of my energy, but I still took off my gi because the humidity in Puerto Rico was just insane. I figured that I only had about 30 seconds to one minute of gas left in the tank. I knew I had to go out there and give everything I had for one minute, and then I'd have to give up.

When Frye and I started fighting, I immediately felt as though I was going to win. After circling for a bit, I threw a couple of punches that missed, and Frye responded by throwing a few punches of his own and then clinching me against the fence. In the struggle to take each other down, we moved away from the fence and I spun around and grabbed Frye from behind, receiving a few elbows to the face for my efforts. Next, I picked Frye up from behind, but because of my lack of experience, I didn't know what to do with him once I had him in the air. I threw Frye forward so that he would drop on his back and I could try and punt his head off his shoulders. It didn't exactly happen as I planned: Frye got up really quickly, and as I was winding up with a soccer kick to send his head to the bleachers, he slipped my kick and I ended up missing.

Smiling, Frye immediately saw his opportunity to capitalize on my mistake and he went on the attack. After closing the distance, he pushed me up against the fence and hit me with some hard right uppercuts, knocking out my mouthpiece. I survived for a bit by hanging onto Frye and was able to pick him up and drop him on his stomach again. I quickly jumped on Frye's back, but I got too far up toward his head and ended up getting rolled. With Frye on top, his experience and confidence overwhelmed me, and I had to succumb to exhaustion. Rather than staying in a position that would leave me vulnerable to a lot of headshots, I tapped out.

When the fight was done, Frye and I embraced in the middle of the Octagon. We were both exhausted and had just been through a war. There were no hard feelings; we were both full of respect for each other as warriors. Before receiving the belt for winning the tournament, Frye asked me if I was all right and then grabbed my hand and thrust it into the air. With both of our hands raised, we turned around and faced the cheering crowd. It was a great feeling. Even though I didn't win, I had accepted the challenge of fighting in the UFC. Without any prior experience, I had made it all the way to the finals.

• • •

After all was said and done, the one thing that I took away from my experience at UFC 8 was that I could earn money in the fight game. In order to ensure that I made as much money as possible, I decided I wanted to mold myself after a fighter who was obviously doing something right from a marketing perspective: Tank Abbott. Tank had trained as an amateur boxer for 13 years before entering the UFC and had a lot of wrestling experience since his dad was a university wrestling coach. However, he was a brawler who loved beating down fighters who had greater martial arts credentials than him.

Tank Abbott was clearly a gifted athlete but what really made him popular with fight fans was his attitude. Tank was a rough customer with a very abrasive disposition. He looked crude and he acted rude. He even called himself a "bully's bully," just one of the little catchy sayings he came up with. Tank was the first fighter who people either loved or really hated. Many other fighters were scared of Tank both inside and outside of the ring. He always brought a large entourage to the UFC events, and there was a widely circulated story that Tank and Paul Herrera had beat another tough fighter named Pat Smith unconscious in a hotel elevator after one of the shows.

Along with being tough, Tank Abbott is known as a man who likes to party. In that sense we're on different sides of the fence, because I don't really like to party. I never really partied after any of my fights. I went there to fight, and when it was done, I went back to my room. I put everything I had into every fight, so there was never anything left; I was always completely exhausted. With Tank, it sometimes seemed as though fighting got in the way of his partying. That said, Tank is a good friend and I love the guy. I'll never forget one time when I was in California out for breakfast with Tank, his girlfriend, and my sister Susie. In the middle of our conversation, Tank suddenly got up and started singing Snoop Dogg's "Drop It Like It's Hot." There we were in the middle of an otherwise quiet restaurant with big, bad Tank Abbott dancing and singing, still drunk from the night before.

Because of all his partying, Tank Abbott has always looked like a big, fat slob. However, Tank's unathletic appearance made him seem like a common man, a blue-collar worker just trying to make a buck, and that helped sell him. Tank was an icon, the first Godzilla or King Kong of mixed martial arts. Royce Gracie was the sport's first icon, but when he had to step aside because of the size and strength of everyone else, Tank took over and the sport started exploding.

In the beginning, mixed martial arts in North America needed a guy like Tank in order to succeed. This is because most early fight fans understood Tank Abbott's explosive striking more than they did Royce Gracie's Brazilian Jiu-jitsu. Educated fight fans definitely understood the intricacies of jiu-jitsu, but the average fan wanted to see somebody get knocked out. Can you blame them? I mean, who wants to look at some guy hugging another man on the floor? There's barely any action. On the other hand, if somebody's getting beat by a better technical fighter and then comes back with a huge knockout, like Tank used to do, that's exciting as hell.

After UFC 8, I took a good look at what Tank Abbott was doing and decided that was what I wanted to do too. Tank was a guy who came out and lost half the time, and yet people still came to every show he was in. Whether he won or lost, everybody wanted to see Tank Abbot. Before I started fighting in the UFC, I didn't care about the money; I thought I wanted to win the competition and be the toughest person around. Following my first UFC, I changed my way of thinking. I knew that I could make a career out of fighting, and I wanted to make money. I reassessed the game and asked myself, *Who was making the money?* Tank Abbott was obviously making money. Royce Gracie and Ken Shamrock were big back then, but they weren't coming back every time. Tank was the only one coming back every time. I wanted the fans to either fall in love with me or completely hate me. I knew I couldn't win every time, but I could convince audiences I was going to fight my ass off each time I got into a battle.

Participating in UFC 8 definitely gave me more confidence in my ability to fight. Up until that point, I was only given a tough name because I was bigger than everybody else. On the inside, I always worried that I was a coward. When I discovered that I could compete against the world's best fighters, I found the thing I had been searching for. Growing up, I always had the burning desire to succeed at something. For a while I thought that I had found my calling in arm-wrestling, but it just didn't feel quite right. Boxing definitely wasn't it, and there was no way I wanted to keep working in a factory. At my first UFC, I found myself. Looking back, the fight with Paul Herrera was the most significant of my career. Had I lost, I may not have had a second chance in MMA. The Herrera fight put me in the spotlight and on track for the rest of my life.

CHAPTER SIX

Shortly after UFC 8, I decided it was time to stop arm-wrestling and focus my time exclusively on mixed martial arts training. I had been arm-wrestling professionally for over 15 years and had reached the pinnacle of the sport. I really didn't think that I had anything more to prove and was ready to make my mark as a fighter. However, before I decided to put arm-wrestling aside completely, an interesting offer came up that gave me the chance to set a world record and to forever mark my place in arm-wrestling history.

One day I was sitting around my house, when a Japanese businessman called me up and asked if I would like to go Japan and arm-wrestle 100 people. He told me his company was throwing an event and that they wanted an arm-wrestling world champion to be there. He wanted to know how much it was going to cost to get me to come. I had to think about it for a minute because I'd never done something like that before. "Well, I don't know," I said. "I guess if you pay for a flight for me, pay for my room and accommodations, and give me $1,000 in daily spending money, then I'd be happy."

Right away he agreed to those terms, which made me wish that I had asked for more. After the price was agreed upon, I was told I would be flying out the following week and staying for three days at the Grand Prince Hotel Akasaka in Tokyo, Japan. One week was really short notice, but I didn't care because I was getting a free trip and $3,000 for only three days of work. At that time, $3,000 was a lot of money for me, so who was I to complain?

Two days before I was supposed to leave for Tokyo, I got a call from another Japanese company asking me how much I would charge to arm-wrestle at their event. Trust me: I thought it was extremely weird for two separate Japanese companies to call me within a week to arm-wrestle, but both offers were legitimate. The stakes were even bigger in the second offer: they wanted me to set a world record by arm-wrestling 1,000 people for a game show on live television.

I remembered how the first company had jumped right away at the price I had suggested. I learned something from that experience, so instead of coming up with a number, I decided I was going to let them name a price. When I asked the company representative to come up with a number, he offered me one million yen just to show up and an additional one million yen if I beat every single person. Back then, one million yen could've been one million pesos for all I knew — I had no idea how much yen were worth compared to Canadian dollars. However, I figured one million in any currency must be a lot of money, so I agreed to the deal. The next day I called the bank to find how much one million yen was. When the lady there told me that one million yen was 14,000 Canadian dollars, I almost fell off my chair. I couldn't believe it — these people were going to give me $28,000 to beat 1,000 people. Once I heard that, I was definitely excited about going to Japan, and I was determined that there was no way I was going to lose to anybody. I got on a plane to Japan the next day.

Both events were huge successes, but the second event was definitely more memorable. During my appearance on the game show, I competed on a big stage in front of a huge, raucous crowd. There were six bodyguards on stage with me and after people arm-wrestled me, the bodyguards would grab them and rip their shirts off. That added some humor to the show and also allowed the organizers to see which people had already arm-wrestled.

That night I ended up beating all 1,000 Japanese people in one hour and 46 minutes. The contract stipulated that halfway through I had to face five people using only one finger, which was hard to do with a tired arm. Regardless, I beat every single person, because there was no way I was going to lose and walk away from the extra $14,000. Setting the world arm-wrestling record pocketed me a good amount of money, but more importantly it gave me a claim to fame and cemented my place in the arm-wrestling history books.

• • •

A few weeks after the Japan trip, UFC President Bob Meyrowitz phoned and offered me $20,000 to compete at UFC 9 in Detroit, Michigan. Bob wanted me to fight Dave Beneteau, a wrestler from Windsor, Ontario, in a fight billed as the "Canadian Championships" to determine the best fighter in Canada. It sounded like a great idea, so I quickly accepted the terms. Instead of another tournament style event, UFC 9 was the company's first full card of pre-determined matchups. The idea of only having to fight one person was quite attractive to me, because it meant that I only had to train for, and worry about, one fight.

Unfortunately, the one fight I had to worry about was with Dave Beneteau. At 6'3", 265 pounds, Beneteau was a tough customer who could easily take somebody down and dominate them. I knew that he was going to present a lot of problems for me, stylistically. Not only was Beneteau a great wrestler, he was a high-caliber striker as well. That ability gave him a step up on other wrestlers because he knew how to strike while he was on the ground. Up until that point, there hadn't really been a wrestler who could inflict a lot of damage on the ground.

The UFC had been receiving a lot of criticism leading up to UFC 9, led by Arizona Senator John McCain, who famously called the sport "human cockfighting." The pressure was so great, it led to an intense legal battle in the Detroit courts when it was announced that the fight was going to be held at Cobo Arena. Right up until the day of the show, it was uncertain as to whether the show would happen. Eventually, the courts decided the show could take place, but with modified rules, such as no closed-fist strikes. Any competitor who didn't comply with the modified rules would be subject to a $50 fine. Before the fight, referee Big John McCarthy told me to try and hit with open palms as much as I could. However, most fighters that night, including myself, punched normally, and none of us were fined.

When I got to Cobo Arena, there was just as much electricity in the air as there had been in Puerto Rico. A lot of people in my hometown had seen my first fight on television and had decided to make the trip from Barrie to Detroit for UFC 9. Even though I was happy to have their support, I ended up hating it, because there were too many damn people, and things got out of hand. I realized that I couldn't have that many people hanging around me before a fight. In order to put on a good performance, I would need to cut out the distractions and concentrate.

I was pumped up to fight Dave Beneteau for the "Canadian Championship," but the match never ended up happening. On the day of our fight, Beneteau broke his hand while sparring with one of his training partners. Beneteau still wanted to fight so he could make money, but the UFC told him that he couldn't, for his own safety. In retrospect, it was a good thing for me that they didn't let him fight: Beneteau probably would have kicked my ass, and I would have looked like an idiot getting beaten by someone with a broken hand.

The UFC replaced Beneteau with his corner man and training partner, former Olympic gold medal wrestler Mark Schultz. Mark Schultz and his brother Dave were powerhouses in the U.S. wrestling scene, each having won NCAA titles and gold medals at the world championships and the 1984 Olympics. Only a few months prior to UFC 9, Dave had been shot and killed by the mentally ill sponsor of his wrestling team,

John E. du Pont. Due to everything he had been through, Mark was very well known. Though I was happy not to be fighting Beneteau, I knew Schultz was no joke either; in fact, he was probably even a bigger threat.

At 5'10", 203 pounds, Mark Schultz was one tough son of a bitch. Along with great wrestling skills, Schultz had also been working on his Brazilian Jiu-jitsu with Renzo Gracie. He could take a strike, which made him difficult to intimidate. Fortunately, fighting Schultz instead of Beneteau didn't affect the game plan at all, since they were both strong wrestlers. I knew I was going to end up on my back, which was where I didn't want to be. There was no doubt in my mind going into the fight that I was going to have a rough time doing what I wanted to do.

When the fight started, Schultz and I came out and circled each other for a bit. We faked some punches and sized each other up before he shot in on me and took me down. As Schultz shot in, I grabbed his head and tried to put him in a guillotine choke; however, when we ended up on the ground, I was only in half-guard, so I couldn't finish the submission. I held on for a bit while Schultz tried to disrupt my breathing by covering up my mouth and softening me up with some punches to the side. When he got out of the guillotine hold, Schultz managed to get side control before I quickly scrambled to my feet.

When Schultz and I got up, we both had blood on us from cuts on his nose and my forehead. The fight didn't stay standing for long. Schultz shot in for a double-leg takedown and got me down again, ending up in my guard. Once he was on top, though, Schultz had a hard time finishing the fight with strikes because I was able to take a punch on the ground, but he did end up cutting the side of my right eye with a glancing blow. Since there was a lot of blood coming from the cut, Big John stopped the fight to wipe the blood off my face with a towel so that the ringside doctor could take a look at it.

I definitely didn't want the doctor to stop the fight from a cut, so I was glad when Big John put my mouthpiece in and told me to get back in there. When we restarted, I threw a jab and then hit Schultz with a leg kick, but I couldn't get off any good, clean strikes. Schultz then aimed a left hook right at the cut above my eye, which surprised me and allowed him to take me down again. On the ground, Schultz worked for a submission from various top positions. By this point I was exhausted and spit out my mouth guard to try and get more oxygen. It wasn't long before Schultz got into full mount and started raining down punches while Big John yelled, "Open hands!" Finally the bell sounded and the fight ended. The rules stipulated that there was supposed to be overtime, but after looking at me during the break, Big John waved his hands and said, "It's over."

I hated losing but was glad that Big John stopped the fight against Mark Schultz. He seemed to know when I had had enough and made a decision that saved me from unnecessary damage. Part of the reason Big John McCarthy has so much respect within the MMA community is because he is fair and does a great job of reading fighters. Big John was a tactical instructor with the Los Angeles Police Department, and anytime I fought, I felt safe if he was the referee. He was big and could stop the match immediately. In fact, later on when I first started fighting in Pride I was scared at first because Big John wasn't there.

My fight against Mark Schultz was just a grind-out war and one of the toughest fights I've had throughout my entire career. It was tough simply because it was the first time I'd fought anybody who was a top-notch wrestler. I basically couldn't do anything against Schultz. I barely threw any punches and kicks and just tried to grapple, which was his game. After my previous experience in the UFC, I had worked a lot on my stamina and left the weights alone, something I shouldn't have done. If I had focused more on improving my strength, I may have been able to dictate more of the fight on the ground. However, even though I made some mistakes, losing to Schultz was not the end of the world. As I told the interviewer after the match, "You've gotta learn how to lose and lose gracefully. I did as well as I could. Now it's back to the drawing board, but we'll come back. No big deal."

UFC 9 taught me something about the fight game that I would encounter again and again throughout my career: wrestlers can start fights but not finish them. Of course, that was back then. Nowadays everybody cross-trains, so you don't run into that problem as much. However, it used to be an issue because strikers like me couldn't solve the problem of the wrestler, and yet wrestlers were unable to finish strikers on the ground. To this day I still haven't really solved the problem of the wrestler; I've just gotten better at avoiding it.

Following my memorable performances at UFC 8 and 9, I was invited back to fight at UFC 10 in Birmingham, Alabama. This time, due to popular demand, the UFC was going back to its tournament format: each competitor would try to win three fights in one night. In the fourth quarterfinal bout of the night, I faced John Campetella, a high school biology teacher from Staten Island, New York. Campetella, a former wrestler who also has a second-degree black belt in Kenpo karate, was barrel-chested and extremely muscular at 5'9", 235 pounds. Campetella was just a giant meatball who probably had muscles in his shit. He was a good kid but, at the time, he was just too heavy for his height.

At the start of the fight, both Campetella and I came out swinging before ending up in the clinch. He hit me with some uppercuts before I pulled guard and wrapped him up so that he didn't have enough space to throw punches. I only spent a short amount of time on the bottom before I swept Campetella and ended up on top. That's when things got nasty and I hit him with three big, unanswered left hands that caused referee Big John to step in and stop the fight. Campetella was mad that the fight was stopped, but it was definitely a good decision because his left eye had completely closed up.

Once I'd made short work of Campetella, I moved on to the semi-finals against UFC newcomer Mark Coleman, another guy who was a top-notch wrestler at the time. A few people had told me that Coleman liked to get into lots of brawls, but other than that, when I first saw this little muscular kid walking around backstage, I really didn't know anything about him. The only thing that I knew was that Coleman's first opponent, three-time Israeli karate champion Moti Horenstein, had submitted by strikes less than three minutes into their first round fight.

I went into the semi-final fight with no game plan at all. Although he didn't really know me either, Coleman definitely had the strategic advantage because he would've seen me in prior UFCs, and he must have known that I was likely to knock his head off.

At 6'1", 245 pounds, Mark Coleman was a stud. An extremely accomplished wrestler, he'd been a two-time all-American wrestler and was an NCAA champion in 1988 with the Ohio State Buckeyes. Following university, Coleman went on to become a two-time Pan American Games freestyle gold medalist, a World Games silver medalist, and a member of the 1992 U.S. Olympic team. Before our fight, Coleman had also been working with Richard Hamilton, the same guy who had helped Don Frye and Dan Severn transition from wrestling to mixed martial arts.

When we started fighting, I rushed at Coleman but he immediately took me to the mat with a double-leg takedown. From that point on, I spent most of the fight just trying to crawl back up to my feet. That was pretty much the story of the fight. Coleman could take me down and get on top of me, but he couldn't do anything to finish me. With the humidity, I was very hot, and Coleman did a good job of tiring me out by smothering my face, posting me up against the fence, and landing a few big head butts. Still, I could've just sat there all day: I was used to getting punched, and it wasn't like Coleman was going to hit me hard enough on the ground to knock me out. On the other hand, I was a good finisher but I couldn't get started. Regardless, Coleman was able to control me and keep me down.

At one point while we were standing, Coleman had my back and I could hear his corner talking to him and giving him advice. I didn't like the advantage that gave him, so I decided to scale the side of the Octagon and bring Coleman into my waters. Once we got to my corner, I was right in front of John Gnap who could help me out with some wrestling advice. John told me to throw some foot stomps and backward elbows at Coleman, who was still behind me, holding on to me with a body lock. Coleman responded by hammering me repeatedly with some hard uppercuts to the face.

When we finally got out of the clinch, I chased Coleman around the Octagon, trying to knock him out and end the fight. However, I couldn't get any clean shots off and Coleman managed to duck under one of my punches and take me down again. He ended up in side control and hit with me with a knee and some right hands. From there, Coleman took my back, flattened me out, and sunk in a rear naked choke, forcing me to tap. I had given it a good go, but at that point in our careers, Coleman was just too powerful and too good of a wrestler compared to me.

Backstage after our fight, Coleman and I started talking and we quickly became good friends. Coleman's not a very talkative person but he's a super nice guy. He's also a party animal. He can drink more than anybody I've ever met and he is the happiest drunk you'll ever meet. Right away we just clicked because we understood each other. Coleman and I got in touch shortly after UFC 10 and started training together. Back in the day, wrestlers needed to learn how to strike and strikers needed to know wrestling. In order to fill those gaps in your game, you'd hook up with somebody who trained in another discipline and teach each other what you knew. Coleman and I never paid each other any money. If he needed training, he'd come up to my place and I'd be his dummy. If I needed training, I'd fly down to Ohio and he'd be a dummy for me.

Aside from providing us with suitable training partners, hooking up with Coleman was also helpful because it gave each of us an experienced fighter to corner our fights. Coleman was always a good corner man because he knew what he was doing and I respected him. He's also great at getting your attention when you're in the middle of a fight. When he's in your corner, you hear nothing but his bellowing voice in your ear. Being a corner man for somebody is a very important job. If you don't know how to corner, you just stay quiet, hand me water, wipe off my face, and put Vaseline above my eyes. A real corner man, on the other hand, needs to know what his fighter can and can't do. There's nothing worse than a corner man coming in there and telling you to do shit that you don't even know anything about.

As a corner man, your main job is to try and look after your fighter. When I'm in someone's corner, I'll always ask him, "Can you hear me?" No matter where you are, whether it's on the bottom, on the top, or standing up, I want to make sure my fighter is listening to my words. They don't have to answer me verbally or even look at me, they just need to nod their head to acknowledge that they can hear me. Once they do that, I can say something like, "I want you to double underhook this guy and take him down to the ground" or "Work toward the arm bar on the left arm" or "You've got 30 seconds left." Usually in a fight, all you can hear is the whole crowd yelling. As a fighter, you need to be able to hear that one voice and pick it out from the crowd. That's why somebody with a booming voice, like Mark Coleman, has been great to have in my corner throughout my career.

Whenever my sister Susie cornered my fights, her job was to do everything I couldn't do. When I couldn't see something, she was there to see it for me. For instance, if I got knocked out in the middle of a fight, I needed somebody there who could make decisions that I couldn't make. Somebody needs to decide whether to cut my arm off or leave it on, or whether to take my eye out or leave it in. I trust Susie with my life. I think everybody in this sport needs somebody who can make decisions that they're going to be able to live with. The only other person I trust like that is Mike Mobbs.

It is important that my corner man makes sure that I am well taken care of when I go to events. Guys like Phil Stoppart and Mike Mobbs were only there for me. The interest that a close friend of mine had when they came with me was completely different from everybody else. For example, I always hated when people I brought tried to get autographs and schmooze. It's all about image, so if you go down there and your guys are getting autographs off somebody else, it doesn't look good. I always wanted the people who accompanied me to act like the epitome of a professional team. When we went to the fights, everybody was representing the team. We would always have a good time but we had to be professional.

My second fight against Don Frye took place on December 7, 1996, at Ultimate Ultimate 96 in Birmingham, Alabama. Ultimate Ultimate 96 was an eight-man tournament held to determine the champion of all champions from past UFC events. I have no idea why they gave me a spot as a champion. I guess it was because I was a runner-up at UFC 8 and another competitor probably didn't show up. In my second fight against Frye, things went down the same way as in our first fight. I blew my wad before I was supposed to, meaning that early in the fight I was completely physically drained. For the entire fight, Frye held me down and just sucked the energy out of me. I had nothing and was forced to tap after he had held me down for over 11 minutes. I had the choice: I could either tap out or I could allow myself to get even more fatigued and let Frye rearrange my face. Frye went on to win the entire tournament in the end. After catching Mark Hall with an Achilles heel hold just 20 seconds into his second fight of the tournament, Frye quickly disposed of Tank Abbott in the finals by a rear naked choke slightly over one minute into the first round. I hadn't won the tournament, but I was satisfied because I had fought the best fighter there and had lasted far longer against him than anyone else had been able to.

• • •

Around the time of my second fight against Don Frye, I was dealing with a lot of personal problems that prevented me from concentrating fully on training and fighting. As most people know, a *personal problem* usually means a *relationship problem* and this time was no different. The relationship I was in at the time was with my now ex-wife Karen Elizabeth Goodridge. I call her "black Karen" because oddly enough, I later married a white woman who was also named Karen Elizabeth.

My first wife and I met on an airplane in 1993 when I was coming back from Nova Scotia after winning the National Amateur Boxing Championship. Karen, a stewardess for Air Canada, was immediately intriguing to me for a number of reasons. Not only was she beautiful with a nice big booty, she also spoke really well and was a very nice person. From the beginning, we saw things along the same lines. The connection was so strong that less than a year after meeting, we got married at a small chapel just outside of Barrie.

Although I loved Karen a lot, our relationship always had a lot of problems. One thing we constantly argued about was money. At the time, I had been in a few UFC fights but wasn't making enough money yet to consider fighting my full-time occupation. Instead, I was training my ass off in the gym for several hours a day and working as a welder at Honda, making $13.45 an hour. Things weren't ridiculously tough, but the truth was I was having a hard time making ends meet.

The reason things were so hard for me was because I was paying for almost everything in our marriage. Even though she was working full-time and we were making the same amount of money, I paid the bills. All Karen had to buy was the food. It wasn't fair, but since she'd moved into my house I had never asked her for money, and that's just what we did. I've always had it instilled in my brain that I have to take care of my family by myself. My job has to pay for everything because I don't want to depend on anyone else.

Since Karen had a lot of extra money floating around, she started paying the bills for her sister, who had just broken up with her husband. The problem was that Karen never discussed with me that she was going to do that. One night we were sitting on the bed together when Karen finally did tell me what was going on. I was furious. It wouldn't have been such a problem had her sister really needed the charity, but that wasn't the case; her sister was the biggest mooch in the world. Karen had been adopted into a white family as a child and for some reason, she always felt like she owed them. Her sister was simply an ass and took advantage of Karen's kindness.

Instead of agreeing to stop letting her sister be a mooch, Karen kept making excuses. The constant excuses got me so angry that all of a sudden, I pushed her off the bed onto the floor. Then I got up and started screaming in her face. In the middle of screaming at her,

I thought to myself, *Holy fuck, you better settle down, Gary.* I knew I had crossed the line. I had always been a gentle giant, but that night I wasn't myself. I don't even remember what happened from first getting angry to standing over top of Karen, about to hit her. After that incident, Karen decided that if she was going to stay with me, I needed to see somebody for my anger. I agreed to do it because I loved her, and I wanted to do whatever I could to save the marriage. Karen was the first person in my life that I had ever felt real love for, and I truly wanted to try and make things work between us.

Entering a men's group for anger management turned out to be a very good experience. To this day it has helped me control my anger by teaching me how to slow things down. I think the reason the group was so successful for me was because it forced me to contemplate some things about my life that I had never really considered before. I couldn't understand how I had gotten angry enough to hurt my wife, because I never thought that I had an anger issue. The reason I never thought I had an anger issue was because I had never been allowed to display anger as a child. Whenever I did, I got my ass beat for it. As a kid, I was only ever supposed to be happy, quiet, and fearful. No other emotions were allowed in our house. I didn't realize until I got older how unhealthy that was for a child. You're supposed to be able to express your emotions in order to learn how to deal with them. The group sessions taught me how to deal with my anger so that I didn't end up seriously hurting someone.

Along with the anger management group, Karen insisted that I also attend a sexual addiction group because she had caught me cheating on her. I never meant to betray Karen, but at the time there was a sexual animal inside me. I was trying to find myself, but because I still didn't know yet who I was, I had to live a lie, meaning that I was telling Karen I was faithful even though I wasn't. That kind of lying was normal to me: I had grown up watching my dad do the same thing. From my dad I learned that you had your wife and then you had other girlfriends on the side. You always kept the two lives separate. I just thought that's how life is. When Karen caught me cheating, I couldn't understand why she came down on me like a ton of bricks. She had me thinking I had serious issues, so I agreed to go to a counselor to help me find out what was wrong with me. I needed to know why I was sexually attracted to so many women. What was wrong with me? Why couldn't I have a monogamous relationship?

I was distraught when I entered the sexual addiction group, but I didn't get very deep into the counseling because I didn't agree with what they were teaching. Everybody was fucking around on his or her spouse, and yet they were telling me I was bad for doing it. The whole situation seemed like it was set up to condemn people without getting to the root of their problems, if there even were any. I remember Janet, the lady who led the group, asking me, "Well, if you're having all this sex, are you wearing a condom?" That question got me frustrated. "Why do you care about that shit?" I wanted to know. "Talk to me about the root of my problem instead of telling me to go out and buy some condoms."

Over and over again, people in the group kept telling me I was setting myself up to lose by having sex outside of my marriage. I didn't agree. To me it was only sex. I wasn't a bad person, I was just naughty by nature. Looking back, I've come to the conclusion that I'm promiscuous because I'm trying not to open myself up to getting hurt. I prepare myself so that when women leave me, I don't care. It's always been easy for me to take that stance, since there are plenty of women out there. If you miss one bus, there are always two more coming.

I never agreed with what was being taught at the sexual addiction classes, but the fact that I attended the group satisfied Karen for a while — at least until she caught me in a lie again. The second time was after UFC 10 in Birmingham, Alabama. The night before my fight against Mark Coleman, I met a smoking-hot girl who was part of the staff at the hotel. She and I started flirting with each other, and when she got off work, I took a taxi over to her house. We had great sex all night. I couldn't get enough of her; she had such a nice body.

When I got back to my hotel room that night, there were tons of messages from Karen waiting for me. The whole time I was out screwing around with this sexy Southern girl, Karen had been calling my hotel room. As soon as I called her back, I could tell she had been crying. When I asked what was wrong, she started crying even harder and wanted to know where I had been all night. I quickly came up with a good excuse that pacified her for the time being: I told her I couldn't be answering the phone the night before a fight; I had to train and sleep. Plus, the other fighters could be calling my room, trying to keep me up all night. The excuse seemed to work, because the tears stopped and it wasn't long before we were back in business. Karen was satisfied, but after having sex all night and then talking on the phone, I was tired as hell. Needless to say, it was not a good way to prepare for a fight.

Karen watched me lose the fight to Coleman on pay per view, and when I returned home, she asked me why I got so tired in the fight. She was fixated on it because in the back of her mind, she thought I had been fucking around the night before when I hadn't answered the phone. But the truth was, fucking around hadn't lost me the fight. The reason I had looked so bad was because Coleman was a top-notch wrestler, and once he got me on my back, I couldn't do anything. I did as much damage control as I could and reassured Karen. She seemed to buy it again and everything went back to normal . . . at least for a little while.

Since the woman I had screwed around with worked at the hotel, she got hold of my phone number and address and called me at home one day. Luckily, Karen wasn't there. Because of her job with the airline, Karen was often gone for days at a time, which was great because it gave me all of the time in the world to have as many other girlfriends as I wanted. But none of my other girlfriends ever called the house. As soon as I heard this girl's voice on the phone, I knew right away who it was and I was furious. "Don't you ever, ever, ever, ever call my house again!" I screamed at her. "I told you I was married and you cannot call my house."

She didn't understand. "Well, you have friends don't you?" she asked. "Can't they call your house?"

"Yeah," I said. "Male friends! If you've got a guy, tell him to call my house. You can't call."

"You're just not like any other guy," she said sadly.

"Yes, I am!" I screamed, trying to make her understand. "Yes, I am. Don't call the house. If you call again, I am in big trouble."

Finally this girl seemed to get it. I beat it into her head so much that she never called again. Perfect, I thought, it was done. Little did I know, it wasn't. This girl may have kept her promise never to phone again, but instead of phoning, she chose to write a letter and send it to my house. At the time, Karen and I always opened the mail together at the kitchen table so we could look at the bills and other things. The day the letter from the Southern girl showed up in the mail, Karen brought in the mail. As soon as I saw the letter, my mind started going crazy. I knew exactly who it was because of the U.S. postage stamp and the woman's writing. How could she have been so stupid? The mysterious letter immediately caught Karen's attention.

For the first time ever, I decided I didn't want to open a letter, and Karen couldn't either. That sent out warning signals to my wife. If I had just taken the letter and ripped it up, it would have been better — I could've said it was a crazed fan. I could have said anything. In hindsight, not opening it was definitely the wrong thing to do. For three days I left it unopened. Every day, Karen asked me, "Gary, why won't you open that letter?"

Finally, while I was at the Honda factory, Karen steamed open the letter and read everything — and I mean everything. The letter was like a five-page novel: *Gary, I'm sorry that I called your house. I know you're married and I don't want your wife to find out, but I will never forget the night that we spent together. You fucked me the best I've ever been fucked in my life. When are you going to come down to see me again?* The entire letter was filled with really explicit details in an effort to try and turn me on so I would visit her again. After she read the letter, Karen sealed it up and put it back where she had found it.

A few days later, when Karen was out, I opened the letter, read it, and then threw it away, thinking that the entire situation was behind me. When Karen got back from work, she started asking again about the night before UFC 10. Since I had no idea she had read the letter, I kept making up excuses until I was blue in the face. Every day we fought about it until I finally started to get really upset. Then suddenly Karen dropped the subject. I didn't hear about it again for almost two months, until I was leaving for the International Vale Tudo Championship in Brazil.

The night before I left for Brazil, Karen gave me so much sex that by the end of the night, I wanted to turn it away. The next morning, there were a lot of kisses and hugs goodbye and Karen and I both talked about how much we'd miss each other. Little did I know, our goodbyes that morning would be our last.

I traveled to Brazil with Dan Severn and his wife Molly, and as soon as we got to the hotel, I tried calling Karen at home. There was no answer, so I waited for a bit and then called a few more times — still no answer. I knew something was going on: Karen was supposed to be at home. Worried, I called my friend Phil Stoppart to see what was going on. As soon as Phil heard my voice, he was upset. "Gary, why'd you have to call me?" he wanted to know. "Why do I gotta be the one to give you the bad news?"

"What are you talking about?"

"Karen's at the house," he said. "She's moving everything out with a couple of her friends and her family."

The news blew my mind. Karen had just given me a sex buffet and now she was moving everything out? I couldn't believe it. I would later find out that Karen had been planning to leave me ever since she read the letter. For months after, she gave me her body and she gave me her love. The whole time she was so secretive about her plans that I had no idea anything was wrong. Thinking about it now, years later, I still can't believe she walked out of the marriage the way she did.

When I found out Karen had left me, I was shocked, but there was nothing I could do about it. I was in Brazil and had a fight to think about. Hanging up the phone, I went and told Dan that my wife had just left me. That was the end of it; it was time to take care of business. After suffering four straight losses to tough world-class fighters, I knew that I really needed to get back on the winning track at the International Vale Tudo Championship (IVC).

. . .

The IVC is a prestigious three-round tournament in Brazil, world famous for having some of the toughest and most extreme fights. The rules of the tournament are simple: there are no rules. Vale Tudo is Portuguese for "no rules." There are no gloves to protect a fighter's hands; basically you can do whatever you want to win the fight. The only illegal moves are biting and eye gouging. Having no rules was not intimidating to me. I was a fighter, so I didn't give a shit about rules. I just wanted to fight.

As soon as I entered the ring for the first time at IVC, I understood that Brazilians are much more passionate about fighting than North Americans. Being in a Brazilian arena is like being in a steaming pot that is ready to boil over. Fighting is such a part of their culture, and at any given moment, Brazilian people want to fight. To understand what fighting in Brazil was like, think of the crowds you see at soccer games. The fans are passionate and boisterous, like hot-blooded pit bulls. When Brazilians watch two humans fighting, it's like they're watching cockfighting: they want to see a lot of blood and violence.

In my first IVC bout, I fought Augusto Menezes Santos. I came out right away and hit Santos with a left hook that sent him falling into the ropes. When he clinched and tried to wrestle me away from the ropes, I grabbed his neck and tried to choke him out with a standing guillotine. I couldn't quite get the choke tight enough, so I trapped both of his arms behind his head and then threw him to the ground, landing on top of him in side control. Then I sat back and shoved his chin down into his chest, almost breaking his neck. Santos couldn't even tap, so he just waved his hands for the referee to save him. I could tell that some of the fans weren't too happy with my submission move, but it didn't matter because I got the quick victory.

After my win over Santos, I faced off against Cal Worsham, a 5'10", 230 pound fighter from California. Worsham, a former marine, was a heavy-weight boxer and a second-degree black belt in tae kwon do. At the time, Worsham was a well-known fighter: at UFC 10 he defeated the much bigger Zane Frazier by TKO and at Ultimate Ultimate 96 he had faced off against Tank Abbott. Going into our fight, I knew that Worsham was just as fresh as me since he had easily beat his first opponent by guillotine choke in 25 seconds. In the end, however, it didn't matter how much energy he had because I completely overwhelmed him.

Worsham started off by clinching and trying to take me down, but I overpowered him and ended up on top. From there I controlled him and hit him with a few body shots before easily passing his guard into side control. Not even a minute into the match, I applied an arm submission called a keylock. Worsham screamed in pain and tapped my back as I torqued his arm, forcing the referee to step in and stop the fight. Afterward, Worsham was in a lot of pain. He definitely tore something and might've even broken his arm.

I went into the finals having fought two matches that lasted just over a minute in total. In contrast, my opponent, Pedro Otavio, had fought for a combined 25 minutes in his previous two fights. I knew that he must be exhausted. I was experienced and confident going into the final and was certain I was going to kick his ass in no time, just like I had done to my first two opponents. But Pedro turned out to be a lot tougher than I expected.

I hit Pedro with some punches and knees right off the bat, but after clinching with him, he tripped me and we fell to the mat with him on top. Pedro was in my guard so I held him close to me, preventing him from posturing up so that he couldn't rain down punches or go for a submission. Eventually, I was able to sweep him and I scrambled to get the fight back standing. Pedro shot in for the takedown and I took his back and fell to the ground with him in a rear naked choke. I couldn't finish the choke and he managed to spin around into my half-guard. Pedro tried to head butt me, and the crowd started chanting his name and reacting loudly to everything that happened. After a bit of a struggle, I ended up in side control. I could hear Mark Coleman in my corner yelling for me to head butt Pedro in the face and hit him with some knees, which I did. When I went for a rear naked choke, I couldn't sink it in again, and Pedro spun around and ended up in my guard.

I was using the guard to keep Pedro at a distance, but I didn't know anything about the guard game at the time. I had only seen other people use it. I improvised by hooking my toe on the top of Pedro's shorts and controlling him by extending and retracting my legs. Anytime I wanted to punch him, I bent my legs and allowed him to come in. Then I would push him out again so he couldn't punch me back.

At one point my foot slipped and came out the back end of Pedro's shorts, making it look like he was shitting my toes. When my foot slipped out of Pedro's shorts, it brushed past his jock and it got me thinking. If I could move Pedro's jock just a little bit to the side, the end of his cup would press up against his penis or balls and cause him a lot of pain. I knew if I could hit Pedro's jock with enough force, it would cut his dick off.

When I got back to my corner after the first round, Pedro's jock was still stuck in my mind. All I could think about was getting it to the side so that I could pinch his dick off. I know that sounds bad, but remember there were no rules, and Pedro was trying to kill me. Against a skilled Brazilian Jiu-jitsu artist like him, I knew I would need a little bit of creativity to win. In the next round, Pedro and I went to the ground again and right away I tried to find his jock so I could crush his nuts. However, this time I just couldn't seem to position it right. Then all of a sudden, even though I couldn't get hold of his jock,

Pedro grabbed his crotch and started screaming as if I was trying to make peanut butter out of his nuts.

It was a farce, and at the time I couldn't comprehend why Pedro would pretend I had injured him. Looking back, I understand he just wanted an easy way out. Pedro was exhausted and getting me in trouble was the only chance he stood of beating me and saving face in front of his hometown crowd. When Pedro started complaining, the referee, Sergio, told him, "Keep fighting. It's not against the rules." As soon as Sergio restarted us, I started attacking Pedro's jock again because I really wanted to damage his stuff. In the end, I won the fight after hitting Pedro with numerous strikes and crumpling him into the corner, forcing the referee to stop the fight. What I thought would be clean and quick was a dirty 16-minute fight.

I got a lot of flak from Sergio for squeezing Pedro's nuts. He even accused me of ruining his show, which made me really angry. "Sergio, obviously you weren't paying attention to what was going on," I said. "You go and get a doctor . . . if there are any scratches or if there is any damage to Pedro's penis, you can keep my money." Of course, I wouldn't have given back the $50,000 for winning if they had found a small scratch on Pedro's dick. However, I wanted Sergio to understand I didn't do any real damage. Pedro had quit because he was too exhausted. None of that matters now, though; I won the tournament and am still an undefeated International Vale Tudo champion.

Ever since I went to Brazil for the first time, I have always loved everything about that country, especially the women. The thing you have to understand is that Gary Goodridge is all about the big booty. When I go to Brazil, all I see are these little tiny waists and these big butts; I love it. One time I told Royce Gracie that I wanted to go to Brazil for the annual Carnival festival. Royce looked at me and said, "Gary, there are two types of people who go to Carnival. There are the people who are going to be robbed and the robbers. Which one do you want to be? Stay home!" How could I? The women there are just too hard to resist.

CHAPTER SEVEN

Soon after I competed in Brazil, I got a call from a Koichi Kawasaki, a man known as Booker K, who would later become prominent in my life. Koichi wanted me to fight for a brand new mixed martial arts organization based out of Japan called Pride Fighting Championships. Koichi told me the event was going to be huge, with the main bout between Rickson Gracie, who many insiders considered the best fighter in the world, and the most famous pro wrestler in Japan, Nobuhiko Takada. When Koichi called me, I didn't know much about the fight scene in Japan, only that Kimo — a strong Hawaiian who had famously given Royce Gracie one of his toughest fights — had fought there and gotten beaten up with head kicks. Kimo was tough, so if he was getting dominated in Japan, the level of competition would be the highest I had ever faced.

I was eager to fight for Pride, so I called my lawyer in New York, Robert Deperge. In the mid-1990s, Deperge was famous for representing many of the top North American mixed martial artists, including Mark Kerr, Mark Coleman, Don Frye, and myself. I first met him at UFC 8 when he was there as Don Frye's manager. Deperge approached me and told me he'd get me more fights. That sounded good to me, so I agreed; that's how he became my manager and he just started pushing me from there. Deperge is a great lawyer who truly seems to care about trying to get fighters the money they deserve. At one point, he even tried to start a fighter's union, which is an idea that has persisted for years but never materialized. Deperge and Koichi hammered out some prices and eventually came up with a figure we were all satisfied with.

Since there had never been a show like Pride before, I had no idea what to expect when I arrived at the Tokyo Dome in October 1997. I couldn't get over the size of the crowd or the amount of people involved in what was going on. Pride was a new organization, but their first show generated a massive amount of media attention. Not only did the event garner large pay per view numbers on satellite broadcasting in Japan, it also attracted a live gate of over 37,000 fans. The reason the event was such an immediate success is because the people behind it knew how to put on an exciting show, with professional wrestling elements like dramatic entrances, fireworks, and loud music. Pride's elaborate theatrics proved that Japanese people are really passionate about mixed martial arts. While the sport is growing in popularity in North America, I don't think it will ever achieve the kind of mainstream support it once had in Japan.

Backstage at Pride, the atmosphere was extremely busy and chaotic. To keep from going crazy, you just have to learn to block out all of the distractions and stay out of the way of everyone else. Before most of my fights, I would usually listen to reggae or sing to calm myself down. As a fighter you have to learn to do *something* to calm yourself down; there's a lot of anxiety and excitement leading up to a fight. I can't imagine how gladiators handled the pressure when they were about to enter a fight to the death. The anxiety and anticipation before battle is just overwhelming. Trying to clear my mind was particularly important at Pride 1 because I was fighting Oleg "The Russian Bear" Taktarov, and he is one tough Russian.

At 6'2", 210 pounds, Taktarov practiced sambo and judo and, as a result, was very slick with submissions. At UFC 6, I had watched him take a beating before catching Tank Abbott in a rear naked choke to win the tournament. After that, he supplemented his submission skills by working on his hands with famed boxing trainer Freddie Roach at the Wild Card Boxing Club in Los Angeles. Taktarov obviously had a lot of skill. Even though I was a little nervous, I didn't let it get to me. When it came down to it, it was just another fight. If I was going to beat Taktarov, I knew that I needed to keep the fight standing and knock him out. I had to stay cool, calm, and collected and make Taktarov pay for any mistakes he made.

Almost immediately after the fight started, I knew I was going to win. Taktarov looked nervous and kept pulling back like he was unsure of himself. I had enough experience to know that when your opponent is pulling back rather than meeting you in the center, you need to keep moving forward. If you do that, you become a much bigger and harder opponent to defeat. After trading a few punches, I opened up a cut under Taktarov's left eye, which gave me even more confidence. I toyed with him by putting my hands down and daring him to punch me. When I hit him with a big right hook, Taktarov dropped, and I jumped all over him. As he tried to get back up, I hit him with another hard punch to the face and he hit the canvas again. I held up after hitting him with a few more punches because Taktarov was turtling up and I thought the referee was going to stop the fight; when that didn't happen, I jumped on him again and hit him with some hard hammer fists to the face.

By this point Taktarov was really busted up, but he was still surviving. I knew I had to finish him, so I hit him with a hard kick to the face that could be heard throughout the arena. As soon as I planted my foot down after the kick, I knew it was broken; since I was in the middle of a fight, however, I had to hide the pain. If I let Taktarov know I was hurt, he would only get stronger. Even after taking a big soccer kick to the face, Taktarov wasn't quite out yet. I was looking for a knockout, so I decided to let him get back up to his feet. When

Taktarov shot in for a takedown, I sprawled and then hit him with some hard jabs. It took a few seconds to find the right opening and then, just under five minutes into the first round, I nailed Taktarov with a big right hook that knocked him out cold and sent him falling to the canvas. It was the first time in my career I had ever knocked out anybody with a punch and it felt great. I was ecstatic because, at that point in my life, it was the biggest fight I had ever been a part of. I had arrived in the UFC with a big bang and now I had done it again in an entirely new organization in Japan.

After the fight against Taktarov, I was so excited about winning that I jumped into the arms of my corner man. Doing so, I realized how much pain my foot was in, so I sat down in the ring for a minute. I told my corner man Stephan I thought I had felt my foot break when I kicked Taktarov in the head. Stephan said, "Aw, don't worry about it, you won," and put some ice on it. Later, I found out that the instep of my foot was, in fact, broken. I didn't know anything about kicking, which meant I had to find out the hard way that I should have kicked with my shin instead of the instep of my foot. If I had kicked Taktarov with my shin, he would've fallen asleep right away. I didn't know that because I'd never trained properly in kickboxing — I just saw an opening to kick Oleg in the face so I went for it. I wanted to win and if a broken foot was the price, it was no big deal.

Following my first fight in Pride, I realized what the organization had wanted to do: build up Oleg Taktarov and make him a superstar in Japan. There were no plans to make a star out of me; I was only supposed to be an organic punching bag brought over to make Taktarov look good. I went into that fight as an underdog who was supposed to lose. Instead, I ended up with a highlight reel knockout over one of the most feared heavyweights in the world. What a way to start my Japanese career.

At Pride 1, I didn't just knock out Oleg Taktarov, I sent him into retirement. He had a couple of wins the next year in a smaller organization, but after I beat him in Pride, Taktarov was never the same fighter. He even decided that it was time to quit mixed martial arts and pursue a movie-acting career. To my surprise, he actually had some success with it and appeared in some Hollywood blockbusters, like *Bad Boys II* and *Predators*.

Ever since Pride 1, I have always enjoyed fighting in Japan. Japanese people have been so gracious to me, and I've fallen in love with the country because of the way they treat athletes. For example, Japanese fans never boo at a fight. I have such a hard time performing for fans who boo. I mean, what the fuck are people booing about? Sure, there may be brief periods where there's a stalemate during a fight, but that's only because two of the world's best athletes are in the ring. There's always a reason when there's a lack of action. Maybe one fighter's afraid to shoot and the other fighter's afraid of getting taken down. Maybe they've been fighting hard and they are resting for a while or trying to psych each other out. Whatever the reason, these athletes work hard and don't deserve to be booed. Don't get me wrong: Japanese fans don't like resting and stalling either; however, they don't show their dissatisfaction by booing. It just rips me apart hearing American fans do it all the time.

The love I have for Japan is mutual. I truly believe the Japanese people enjoy my heart, my fighting charisma, and my samurai spirit. I have a no surrender, no mercy attitude. I just keep going balls to the wall, and it doesn't matter whether I get hit or hurt. Whatever happens, I just keep going, which is a fighting quality Japanese fans really appreciate. While only fight fans know about me in North America, I'm a household name in Japan. If a Canadian person recognizes me from TV, they might say, "Oh, hey Gary. What's going on, buddy?" Or they might just whisper to their friends about me or pretend that they don't know who I am. When I would go to Japan, however, people would stop their cars in the middle of the road and ask me to come over for pictures. In that country I was like a rock star. It wasn't unusual for people in Japan to run after me in the streets to sign their shirts or their little autograph books. Almost all of the fans who came up to me took my picture with their cell phones. Often, they'd even call other people and ask me to talk to their friends or family. The Japanese people are absolute fanatics like that and love everything about celebrities. We were a perfect match for each other.

• • •

When I signed that first contract with Pride and beat Oleg Taktarov, I knew that I had made it in the fight game and would be around for a while. Finally I would be able to make a career out of fighting. The problem was that in order to start training again, I had to wait for my broken foot to heal. In all, it took six weeks for my foot to heal properly. Being injured for so long was one of the reasons I ended up getting fired from the Honda auto plant. The reason they gave was that I stole a hotdog from the cafeteria, but I believe it was all about complaints and jealousy. I was well known at Honda from arm-wrestling and fighting, and since I was the only big black man working in a white community, I was like a fly in a bowl of milk. In factories, people are always jealous of other people who are successful at doing something outside of work. Many of my coworkers saw me making extra money fighting and arm-wrestling. Sometimes I'd come back and have to be on modified work because I was injured. The whole situation created a lot of resentment and jealousy. I was not welcome at Honda, so they came up with a reason to get rid of me, which was fine with me. Pride had already called me to compete at their second event, so I had a fight to think about.

My first fight with Oleg Taktarov had been tough, but he was a little bit overrated as a fighter. In Pride 2 I was set to face Marco Ruas, who I knew was a great fighter with a dangerous submission game. Ruas was called the "King of the Streets": *rua* means street in Portuguese, and Ruas was from the streets of Rio de Janeiro. Going into the fight, I actually thought Ruas was going to beat me because he had a lot of hype around him after winning the UFC 7 tournament and garnering victories over standouts like Keith Hackney, Steve Jennum, and Patrick Smith.

When we finally started fighting, I surprised myself by almost tearing Ruas up. He tried a few things like a roundhouse kick and a spinning back fist, but it wasn't long before I had him backed into a corner. I was landing some hard punches so Ruas shot in on me, but when we ended up on the ground, I was in side control. Once Ruas moved to half-guard, I was able to hit him with some hard punches from the ground, which opened up a cut on him. Leading up to Pride 2, I had been working a lot on my submission game. I really wanted to test out my new grappling skills, so I tried for a leg lock and then a neck crank but couldn't quite lock them up. Ruas was also going for a lot of submissions, but I was controlling him from top position and stopping all of his attempts. I let Ruas stand back up, but when we moved into the corner I slipped and hurt my leg. Immediately, Ruas took advantage of the opportunity and hit me with some punches to set up a take-down. During the takedown I ended up on top but right away Ruas caught me in a heel hook. As soon as Ruas turned and cranked my leg, I had to submit. I couldn't believe it. I had given Ruas a good beating the entire fight, but at the very end, he squeaked out an ankle lock and won by the hair on his chinny-chin-chin. I was devastated.

Following my loss to Ruas, I was really looking forward to getting in the ring again to try and please the Japanese fans with an exciting and entertaining win. I knew I had to make a good impression on the fans and show them I was a fighter who was here to stay. Originally I was supposed to go up against Kimo at Pride 3, but he tore his knee shortly before the fight and had to pull out. A fighter named Amir Rahnavardi had traveled to Japan to be in Kyle Sturgeon's corner, and when Pride officials asked Amir if he would fight as Kimo's replacement, he agreed. Amir was a submission fighter from California with a reputation for being a good, tough opponent. I wasn't worried about losing, though. I was supremely confident in my abilities and thought I was going to tear Amir a new asshole.

At the beginning of the fight, Rahnavardi hit me with some punches to the face and I just smiled because I knew he had nothing. When we clinched, I kneed Amir to the body and hit him with some more punches. Amir quickly realized he didn't want to exchange with me on our feet and went for a leg sweep. He got my feet out from under me, but I was able to shift momentum and end up on top of him. While Amir tried desperately to tie me up, I kept hitting him with punches.

The fight with Amir was particularly memorable because we talked smack to each other and played mind games throughout the entire fight. Amir was a very spunky, young, spry kid whose balls were just way too big for him; I had to bring him down to size. When I was on top hitting him, he would say things like, "Oh, that didn't hurt. You hit like a pussy." I knew what he was trying to do. He was trying to intimidate me and talk his way to a win, rather than fight his way there. You have to learn to deal with those types of things because many fighters come in with different styles and techniques. Trying to mess with your opponent's mind can be a good strategy that takes him off his game. Amir would tell me to go ahead and hit him and when I would, he'd fake a scream like it hurt and then call me a wimp.

Amir was acting like he wasn't getting hurt, but I was hitting him with hard, loud punches to the head and body. He rolled and tried to get me in a heel hook followed by a knee bar. Fortunately for me, I had been in a similar situation against Ruas and had worked on leg lock defense between fights. After getting out of the heel hook, I ended up in top control. When I postured up, Amir went for a triangle choke, but I was too strong and powered my way out of it. I tried for a couple of submissions, but mostly I wanted to pound Amir's face in.

Amir had been talking smack earlier in the fight; now it was my turn. When he tried to punch me from his back, I said, "That's a sissy punch," and he laughed. After that, I let him hit me and really got into the smack talk. I started begging him to hit me because I knew that I was about to fill in his face with my knuckles. I got him with some hard rights from his guard and managed to trap his left arm under his body, leaving him with only his right arm to defend himself. I saw my opening and loaded up a big right hand that knocked Amir out cold. I hit him with two more hard rights before the referee stepped in and deflected the last punch at 7:22 of the first round.

After the fight was over, I raised my hands in the air and yelled, "I love you!" to the crowd. It felt good to be back in the winning column again. It also felt good to have given the Japanese crowd another exciting and entertaining fight. To this day, a lot of people still remember the friendly trash-talking between Amir and me. That's probably because there are hardly any other fighters out there who talk trash during a bout. You've got so many things on your mind, you can't afford to start getting distracted with insults. Even still, in certain situations, trash talk can be the perfect ingredient for an exciting fight, and it definitely made my fight at Pride 3 memorable.

• • •

In early 1999 I got a call from the UFC asking me to fight again, and I quickly accepted. UFC 19: Ultimate Young Guns, held in Bay St. Louis, Mississippi, was set up as a tournament to determine the heavyweight champion after Randy Couture had vacated the title. My fight at UFC 19 was an exhibition match against Andre "The Chief" Roberts. At 6'4", 410 pounds, Roberts was an incredibly massive Native American. When I saw him I was afraid, but I knew there was no way I could allow Roberts to beat me. I had already developed a good reputation in the fight world, but I had also suffered some losses. I figured that if I lost to Roberts at this point, my career would be done.

I had no idea how I was going to beat Roberts at UFC 19. He had been training with Pat Miletich, a legendary trainer and fighter in his own right. Since the Miletich Fighting Camp was renowned for producing tough scrappers who were hard to finish, I figured I was in for a long brawl. Roberts was a boxer, so I knew I was going to have problems going toe to toe with him because he's taller than me and has a reach advantage. He was also a wrestler, so I knew I would also have problems taking him down. Even if we got to the ground, he was strong as hell and had dangerous elbows. I needed to be quick in order to tire him out. Going into the fight, I didn't care about anything other than being fast.

Everything I did seemed to work perfectly. I hit Roberts at will with straight shots and nailed him with some hard left and right hooks. I did what every little guy has to do in order to fight a giant — sticking and moving and hitting him with quick punches and kicks. Roberts tried to corner me in the cage but couldn't catch me, because I was too quick. When I hit Roberts with a few really hard shots about 40 seconds into the fight, he turned his back to me and ran away shaking his head before tapping out on his own leg.

Following the fight, Roberts said that I had broken his nose, and that it felt like his nose was going through his brain. Of course, all of that was a bunch of crap: he just didn't want to get hit anymore. Roberts was a very nice guy and I really liked him, but the reality is he quit. He ran away and patted his ass like the biggest wimp I'd ever seen. I couldn't believe it. After what he did, I don't respect him as a fighter.

Along with the heavyweight tournament and exhibition matches, UFC 19 also featured a number of middleweight bouts. One of those was the UFC debut of the now legendary Chuck "The Iceman" Liddell. Chuck's a pretty cool guy and I've met him on several different occasions, although we've never fought each other because of our weight difference. His fight that night was a big deal because he had been trying to get into the UFC for a long time, but they wouldn't let him for some reason. Chuck lost at UFC 19 to the much more experienced Jeremy Horn, but he proved that night he could bang with the big guys.

One of the main reasons people remember UFC 19 is because that was when the feud between Ken Shamrock's Lion's Den and Tito Ortiz started. The problem began after Tito beat Lion's Den fighter Guy

Mezger and then put on a shirt that read "Gay Mezger is my bitch." I love both Guy Mezger and Tito Ortiz because they're both super nice guys and good fighters, but that ordeal was not as big as it was made out to be. Backstage there was no noticeable tension at all. Those guys were only trying to sell tickets and do what they had to do to make money for their families. Tito's an interesting character and he was always trying to take his opponents off their game by wearing shirts that had controversial statements on them. Audiences want to see Tito Ortiz get his ass kicked, and that's how he makes his money.

After UFC 19, I never fought in the UFC again. Instead, I focused on developing my career in Japan with Pride. There weren't any bad feelings between the UFC and me; it was just time for me to move on. As it turned out, my decision to stick with Pride was a good one because mixed martial arts in the U.S. was about to enter a period known to fans as the "dark ages." Thanks to John McCain's campaign against the sport, the UFC was dropped from its pay per view and home video distributors, and the staging of mixed martial arts events was banned in 36 states. It wasn't until years after I left that Zuffa purchased the company and started the long process of mainstreaming MMA in North America.

CHAPTER **EIGHT**

Whatever was going on with the UFC, there was always a home for me at Pride. For the most part, Pride was really well organized and always seemed to keep the focus on the fighters. Naoto Morishita and other members of the Pride staff became like a second family to me. It was always a great organization that treated my family and me first class all the way. Pride was also a good fit for me because the Japanese public really embraced me and was quite interested in what I was up to. Maybe *too* interested: Japanese paparazzi would sometimes show up at my place in Barrie. I'd see them as I was leaving the house, and we'd usually set up a time to have an interview. I always thought it was pretty neat and never worried about my family's safety; these guys were harmless and very friendly. In Japan everything was multiplied by at least 10. When I was in Japan, everybody would try to touch me or get a look at me or talk to me. It was quite humbling, actually.

One thing I really liked about fighting in Pride was the fact that they paid me with a briefcase full of cash after the fights. The last thing that I wanted was a check because it meant that until I cashed it back in Canada, I'd be wondering if I would actually get paid. If, for whatever reason, the check bounced or didn't go through, then what was

I going to do? Who exactly was I going to take to court? Since I lived outside of Japan I always preferred to be paid in cash, because otherwise they've got your nuts over the barrel. The flipside, of course, is that cash is hard to get across the border. You've got to sneak it on the plane because nobody is going to let you into the country with a ton of cash without making you answer a million different questions. It made for some hairy situations.

There's always a lot of talk among fans about whether certain fights in Pride were fixed. Some people don't like to admit that kind of stuff goes on in mixed martial arts, but it does. Sometimes a fighter's camp will come up to you backstage and ask how much it would cost to have you stay away from certain aspects of the fight in order to give their guy a better shot. For instance, they might want you to avoid a fighter's sore knee. I remember being asked by the corner of an opponent who had a weak chin what it would cost not to punch their fighter in the head. I didn't take the deal because I knew that I didn't stand any chance of winning if I couldn't punch to the head. I'm not a submission expert, so if I'm not going to punch you in the head, chances are I'm not going win. Sure, I could try and break a rib or something, but that's a pretty hard way to stop a fight.

As another example, if a fighter was an excellent kickboxer the opposing corner might ask what it would cost not to kick their fighter's leg. You have to be careful, though, because sometimes when people ask you to do something like that, they were trying to lead you in a particular direction. Maybe their fighter was completely healthy and they were misleading you, trying to make you think your opponent had an injury so that you would change your game plan. Sometimes it wouldn't even be the corner asking; it would be an opponent himself. It was all a bargaining system — if you negotiate properly, you can buy anything. The public usually doesn't find out about that type of stuff because it was understood among fighters that those types of dealings were very private. Nobody talks about it because it's embarrassing and robs the sport of legitimacy, even though it happens just as much in other sports like hockey and football.

Another experience I had with attempted fight fixing was before my fight with Naoya Ogawa at Pride 6. Ogawa was an Olympic silver medalist in judo and a former professional wrestler. However, despite his grappling pedigree, he was not on the same level as me as a mixed martial artist. The guys in Pride were hoping to make Ogawa a home-grown star, but they knew I was probably going to beat him. In order to try and make him seem like a legitimate mixed martial arts fighter, his corner men quietly came up to me before our fight and offered me $20,000 to take a dive. I told Ogawa's corner I didn't want any money, because I wasn't going to lose to him. Of course, that turned out to be the stupidest thing I've ever done — I ended up losing to Ogawa anyway. His team just wanted to ensure victory, probably because there was some behind-the-scenes betting going on. Ogawa was on an upward swing in the Japanese professional wrestling ranks, and his people wanted to keep him there. I thought that if I did beat Ogawa, my salary would be increased considerably.

Before our match, the crowd was slowly shouting "O-ga-wa" over and over again. Clearly, I was going to have to take the fight to the hometown favorite in order to get the Japanese crowd to root for me. As soon as the bell rang, I immediately went after Ogawa, hitting him with some big punches that stunned him and had him turning away, just trying not to get hit. He went for a takedown, but I just shoved him off me and went after him again. Ogawa tried to keep me at bay with a defensive front kick, but I closed the distance and landed some huge uppercuts and hooks. Ogawa tried covering up by bending over with his hands up by his head, so I started delivering some knees from the clinch.

Despite the hard shots I was landing, Naoya Ogawa was tough and he managed to come back and hit me with a few hard punches. When Ogawa got double underhooks, he took me to the ground. From my half-guard, he went for a keylock and had the submission locked up pretty tight. I could hear the referee yelling at me, "Give up? Give up?" but there was no way I was tapping. Ogawa couldn't quite secure the keylock so he tried again. At that point, I bucked my hips and managed to sweep him, ending up on top. Ogawa had an active guard and attempted a few submissions like a triangle choke and a keylock again on my left arm. As I got out of the submission attempts and was standing over top of Ogawa, he tried to kick me so I grabbed his leg and fell back, trying to sink in a knee bar. I couldn't quite get it though and Ogawa ended up in side control. After failing at another keylock attempt, Ogawa hit me with some hard hammer fists, which forced me to give my back up to him. Ogawa hit me with more punches while he was trying to take my back, but he couldn't quite get his hooks in. Instead, he took the mount and then transitioned to the side mount, threatening a straight arm bar. By the time the bell rang to end the first round, my lip was busted up and Ogawa had a cut on the bridge of his nose.

The second round didn't last very long. After we exchanged punches for a bit, Ogawa got me down and finally got the keylock he had been trying to secure throughout the fight. The submission was deep and I had no choice but to tap out on his forehead or Ogawa would have snapped my arm. I've never broken a bone from not tapping. You pretty much know when to tap because you know when your opponent has got you good. If you don't want to tap, you've got to count on having a good referee there to stop the fight before it gets to the point where you break something. Some fighters really do try to mess you up but in general, most fighters will give their opponent a chance to tap before they fully crank a submission.

Going into our fight, I definitely underestimated Ogawa. He was a tough guy, but there was more to the story than that. Here's what happened. Sakakibara, who was running the Pride organization, came up to me before the fight and said, "Listen, Gary, I want you to win this fight. You win this fight and you write your ticket into this organization. We will give you the sun, the moon, the stars, the sky . . . everything."

Of course, this was the day of the fight when he was telling me this stuff, so it got me really excited. Then Ogawa's corner wanted to pay me to lose to him. At first I was confused and didn't know what to do, but it didn't take me long to figure out what I had to do. I had to kick Ogawa's ass for my company. Sakakibara had pumped me up so much I was really hungry going into the fight. I wanted to kick Ogawa's ass so bad that I went crazy out there and ended up blowing my load in 30 seconds. I went for a sprint, which is fine if you're effective at what you're doing. The problem was that I'd never sprinted before, and I completely exhausted myself and had nothing left by the end of it.

In hindsight, I should have taken a dive in the Ogawa fight because I ended up getting the loss anyway. The problem is people look phony in fixed matches. I mean, look at the match at Pride 5 between Mark Coleman and Nobuhiko Takada. Takada was the same former professional wrestler who had lost to Rickson Gracie at Prides 1 and 4. Takada was another guy the Japanese wanted to make look like a legitimate fighter. However, the truth was that Takada couldn't even beat the dangles in Coleman's underwear. Right at the end of their match, Coleman astoundingly switched from side control to the lesser position of full guard and then basically gave Takada his leg for the heel hook. It was such bullshit, and you could see it a mile away. I understand why people take dives — the sport of mixed martial arts is entertainment and the point is to make money. I just didn't want to take a dive because I didn't want a loss on my record at the time. I wanted to be in the game and still hold onto my integrity. I didn't want to lose who I was just for a buck.

• • •

Another controversial aspect of fighting in Pride was the use of steroids. Pride fighters always looked big, and the drug testing in Japan wasn't as rigorous as it was in other places. A lot of people make a big deal about fighters getting caught using steroids, but let me tell you something about fighters: many of them take special anabolic drugs to make themselves run faster, have better cardio, and become bigger and stronger. It's not just the guys who *look* like they're on steroids who are doing the drugs, either. Sometimes the guy who looks like a regular Pillsbury Doughboy is doing more juice than the one who looks like he's cut from granite. Look at Josh Barnett. Where is his muscle? Does he even have any? And yet, he was caught using the juice. He even got kicked out of the UFC and stripped of his heavyweight title for using steroids.

Speaking of Barnett, when I first met him, I didn't like the best bone in his body. I thought he was arrogant and immature. I usually really like people when I first meet them, but some people just have to grow on you, and that's the case with him. Barnett is a good man, and he means well. I think I gave him the wrong shake the first time around. Now we basically have a good relationship — I respect him as a fighter and he respects me. He's a top five fighter for heavyweights. He had a really good teacher in Erik Paulson, who was considered one of the best grapplers in the world. I think people point their fingers at Barnett too much because he got a raw deal with the UFC, and I feel bad for what he went through with all that steroid crap.

People who tell you that they don't cheat are liars. I'm of the belief that if you don't cheat, you're not trying. If you're not willing to cheat to win, then what the hell good are you as a fighter? Even if a fighter is not doing steroids, he's cheating somehow. People use the fence to pull themselves into a better position, or they'll give an extra elbow shot or hit after the bell. There's such thing as proper cheating and then there's just being dumb. The question is: to what extent do you cheat and what kind of cheating is it? I know it's the wrong thing to say and it's the wrong thing to teach your children, but once you get this in your head, you'll understand that it's the reality of life — everyone cheats.

Following my upset loss to Naoya Ogawa, I fought Tom "The Big Cat" Erikson at Pride 8 in Tokyo, Japan. Tom is 6'3" and says he's 280 pounds, but in reality, he's over 300. Erikson, an assistant coach with the Purdue wrestling program, was a serious heavyweight wrestler, a two-time all-American, a four-time Olympic qualifier, and the winner of numerous international wrestling competitions. Only a few months prior to Pride 8, Erikson and I had met each other for the first time at a show in Montreal. We had seen each other fight before, so right away we started sizing each other up. We were both kind of nervous to meet each other, because there were very few heavyweights at the time and we knew that we were going to end up fighting.

Going into our fight, Erikson was undefeated in mixed martial arts, so I knew he was going to be tough. In fact, Erikson was my toughest fight up until that point. Erikson is freaking amazing, but it was no big deal standing across from him in the ring. I've fought bigger, faster, and more muscular guys. I've never been intimidated by anybody. Once you're intimidated by somebody, it's probably a good time to get out of the game. We both came out and started beating on each other right away. Erikson landed some big uppercuts and right hooks early on, but when I started to answer back, he drove me into the ropes and took me down. After trying to get a side choke and an arm lock from side control, Erikson got the mount and started raining down heavy hammer fists on my face. I could hear my corner yelling, "He can't hurt you, Gary. You've got the tools." It was encouraging, but the truth was Erikson's hands felt like cement bricks. Those were the hardest punches I've ever felt in any fight; it seemed like every punch was damaging my face and caving in my bones. It was the first time I had somebody on top of me who could've finished me. His hands were just so bloody heavy.

It doesn't take a genius to know that I didn't want to be in that position very long. Erikson was like a giant, heavy rug I couldn't get out from under. I decided to carry on like his punches didn't hurt. I started taunting him, "Hit me. Hit me, baby, please." Then I started making kissing noises and asked, "How about a kiss?" When Tom hit me again, I asked, "Can't you hit harder than that?" The next time he hit me, I sarcastically yelped, "Ow, ow, ow." I guess the strategy worked, because Erikson stopped punching me and starting working for a Kimura, which he couldn't get by the time the round ended. I was exhausted after the first round but I was trying to mess with Erikson's mind, so I walked around the ring like I was full of energy. In the end, it didn't make much difference because Erikson took me down again in the second round and held me there until the end of the fight. Even with the loss, I was pleased because Erikson had finished all of his previous opponents, but he hadn't been able to finish me.

After our fight, Erikson and I started hanging out — he actually ended up cornering my very next fight. From the moment we met, Erikson has always been a gentleman, and we became quick friends. Along with being in my wedding party, Erikson accompanied me to a bunch of places like Japan, Korea, and Russia, strictly because he wanted to help and support me in my fights. Erikson always made sure I was comfortable and looked after at fights, which I'm very thankful for. He is a much better person than me, and I don't really consider very many people better than me, because I'm pretty good. Tom Erikson is a man among men.

I've always respected Erikson because he was willing to fight anybody, anytime. What most fans don't know is that fighters pick and choose who they want to fight. I never understood that. I mean, what the hell? We're fighters! You're supposed to be a tough son of a bitch, but you don't want to fight certain people? Erikson and I are two of the only people in this business who will fight anybody, any style, anytime, anyplace. Give either one of us a week's notice and we're there. We're not trying to pad a win-loss record; we're just trying to fight. We just want to beat people up and make money. Erikson is also not trying to have any long fights. In that way, he's the same as me. You only get paid for the first minute of a fight — after that it's overtime. Who wants to do work and not get paid?

Throughout his career, Erikson got screwed over because of his size and his skill level — nobody wanted to fight him. Everybody in the heavyweight division avoided Erikson, but I never avoided anybody. Ask any heavyweight out there right now if they wanted to fight Erikson and they'll say no. Ricco Rodriguez and Mark Kerr even had it put specifically in their Pride contracts that they would fight anybody but Tom Erikson, and they weren't the only ones. The reason is simply that Erikson's just a top-notch wrestler and he's so damn big. On top of that, I helped teach him some striking, so everybody was extra afraid of him.

• • •

In early 2000, my first child, Trinity Goodridge, was born. Trinity's mother is Charlie Austin. Back in 1998 I was driving along the beachfront when I saw this beautiful woman with long, curly brown hair. I couldn't believe how beautiful this woman was — I almost broke my neck trying to get a look. I pulled over really quickly and turned my car around because I had to see who she was. It was Charlie Austin, a friend I had grown up with. I had never looked at her in a sexual way before. Ever since the day I saw her walking along the beach, however, I started to look at her differently.

After Karen left me, I lived with Charlie, and we decided to have a child together. If it didn't work out between us, we agreed I would pay for the child. From the get-go, our relationship was up and down. Charlie had a messed-up childhood, and we shared a lot. We were more friends than lovers. She was there for me and I was there for her. I didn't love Charlie but I really liked and respected her. That's why I decided to have a child with her.

It was late in Charlie's pregnancy that I went to Japan for 10 days to compete in the opening round of the Pride Grand Prix 2000. The baby wasn't due for another three weeks.

Pride Grand Prix 2000 was an open weight tournament, held at the Tokyo Dome, to determine the best fighter in the world, pitting 16 men against each other for a chance to compete in the eight-man final round event. Since the victor of the tournament won $200,000, the Grand Prix drew all of the top fighters in the world, including Kazushi Sakuraba, Mark Coleman, Igor Vovchanchyn, Mark Kerr,

Royce Gracie, and myself. Going into it, I figured I had a puncher's chance to win, but since I didn't really know anything about submissions, it was going to be hard. However, in my mind, I still convinced myself I was the favorite to win. As a fighter, you have to believe that you're the favorite, otherwise you don't stand a chance.

Usually there wasn't much time to think about it, because I would often get called in as a replacement fighter only 10 days before an event took place. Once a fight was booked, I'd have to get a travel visa together quickly and try to get in a few days of training. Most of the time, I'd use the same travel agent to book the flights, which were always first class. At the airport in Tokyo, there'd usually be one or two other fighters arriving at the same time as my crew, so we'd all travel together on a shuttle bus to the Hilton. Once I had settled into my room, I would sort out my day. Pride would give me an itinerary of press conferences and meetings I would have to attend.

On fight day, the atmosphere at the Pride Grand Prix 2000 was intense. All of the fighters were filled with anticipation, which made the bus trip to the fight unusually quiet. The bus rides normally have a party atmosphere with people talking and laughing. However, this time, everybody was focused and ready to go. The Tokyo Dome is a great place to hold an event like the Grand Prix. Not only is it huge, it was extremely clean and organized. Each fighter got a Japanese lunch box, and the catered food was great. Before the fights, Pride made sure the fighters had everything we needed.

Before I fight, I try to relax and make sure that everything is as calm as possible. By the time I would walk down the ramp to the ring, all of my doubts, if there were any, needed to be gone. I had to forget about any injuries that might be bothering me. I always tried to think about what my first move in the fight was going to be. I didn't want to wait and see what my opponent was going to do. I'm not a counter puncher, so I like to have a plan as to what exactly I'm going to do.

In the opening round, I faced off against Osamu Tachihikari. At 6'5", 297 pounds, Osamu started his career as a sumo wrestler and had since become very popular in Japan as a professional wrestler. When the fight began, I attacked Osamu with a low kick and then hit him with some punches and knees to the head. I had Osamu a little bit rocked so I decided to take him down and punish him on the ground. While I was in side control, Osamu was trying to hold on to me to stop me from posturing up, so I put my forearm across his throat and pushed down. To my surprise, Osamu tapped out less than a minute into the first round. The forearm choke is something nobody should ever be choked out with, but when new fighters get a forearm in the throat, they just panic. They can still breathe but they end up tapping out because things are starting to get painful and they are worried. It felt good to beat Osamu, but I was actually quite surprised that I beat him so easily.

As soon as the fight was over, I went back to the hotel and was shocked to get a message from Charlie that she was in labor. I called her right away to see how she was doing, and she told me that she was getting ready to go to the hospital. I had taken the doctor's timeline literally; I've since learned that there's no exact prediction on when a baby is going to be born. I had wrongly expected that the baby was going to wait for me to come home. Charlie had to get off the phone to get to the hospital. I called Mike Mobbs, but he was already on the way to the hospital as well. I waited for a little bit and then called Charlie back so that I could try and be with her. Throughout that night and the next morning, I spent the entire labor and delivery on my phone talking to Charlie. It ended up costing me $2,400 for a 12-hour call from Japan to Canada, but it was worth every penny. I'm glad I didn't get the phone call from Charlie *before* I fought, because I don't think that I would have done so well knowing that she was going through labor without me.

Being a father completely changed my life. Mike Mobbs used to tell me all the time that I wasn't going to know what love was until I had a child. At the time, I had issues with the concept of love. I mean, I knew that I loved my sisters and my mom, but that's not the same kind of love. When Trinity was born, I finally knew what unconditional love was. When I got home from Japan and met my little girl, I stayed up all night just looking at the prettiest thing I had ever seen. She may have been wrinkly and red, but she was beautiful.

. . .

My win over Osamu Tachihikari earned me a spot in the Pride Grand Prix 2000 final bracket, which took place three months after the first event. In the quarter-finals that night, I faced off against the "Lethal Weapon of the North" Igor Vovchanchyn, from Kharkov, Ukraine. The fight was a rematch, since we had already faced each other at Pride 4 in between my fights with Amir Rahnavardi and Andre Roberts. At 5'9", 220 pounds, Vovchanchyn was a little sawed-off fireplug who was built for fighting. He began his career as a kickboxer and, as a result, his strikes were extremely fast by mixed martial arts standards. When Vovchanchyn started in MMA, he quickly won four eight-man tournaments in Russia. After his incredible success in Pride, he was considered one of the favorites to win going into the Grand Prix.

Though I knew he hit like a truck, I thought I could handle Vovchanchyn. Early in our first fight at Pride 4, I got double underhooks and took him down. On the ground, I went for a heel hook but couldn't finish, and Vovchanchyn ended up getting on top. I gave him my back in an attempt to stand up, which I managed to do. I didn't want to test Vovchanchyn standing so I took him down. After a bit of ground and pound, he was bloodied up from a cut, so I stood up over top of him and asked the Japanese referee, "Can I kick face? Can I kick face?"

"No, no, no," the Japanese referee said. "No kick face."

After letting Vovchanchyn up, we clinched and exchanged a few punches. Then, out of the blue, he landed a huge straight left followed by a big left hook that just floored me. I fell back and hit the ropes, and the referee stepped in to stop the fight. I didn't even see the punch that knocked me out coming. I woke up after it was all over and was pissed that I had gotten caught.

I knew I had had a good showing against Vovchanchyn up until the knockout, and I didn't want to have to listen to this guy again, so I was determined to win our rematch at the Pride Grand Prix. The quarter-final fight was my chance for revenge, and I was sure I could catch Vovchanchyn and knock him out. My plan was to be patient and keep him on the end of my punches because he had a smaller reach and further to go in order to land a punch.

After Vovchanchyn and I touched gloves in a show of respect, the fight started. From the opening bell, it was just two brawlers going at it, which made the fight a classic. Early on, we were just feeling each other out with jabs, but it wasn't long before we started letting our hands go. When I got Vovchanchyn in a Muay Thai clinch and tried to throw some knees, he countered with some good combinations. Following the exchanges, Vovchanchyn threw a big knee that hit me square in the groin. Immediately, he backed away and bowed to apologize and show me that he hadn't meant the illegal blow.

I could feel that my jock had caved in, so the referee called a timeout for me to get another cup. I had to leave the ring and change my jock in front of everybody, while some Pride workers held up white sheets around me so the crowd couldn't see. Looking back, it was pretty funny to get kicked in the nuts in front of 70,000 Japanese people who were all laughing at me. As it turned out, when the jock caved in, it grabbed my testicles. Then when it popped back out, my scrotum was locked in it. I got some help opening up the jock and taking my scrotum out, at which point I could see that there was a lot of damage to my testicles. When the jock was finally taken off, I wanted to cry and scream, but people were watching and I couldn't act like a little kid. I had to carry on like nothing was wrong because I was in the middle of the fight. Luckily, I didn't need surgery, just a lot of ice and TLC. Needless to say, after that incident, I switched from a plastic jock to a steel one.

When I got back in the ring and the fight resumed, Vovchanchyn and I were both moving in and out and blocking punches well. When he threw a high left hook that landed, I shook it off to show him it didn't hurt. I even stuck out my chin to try and bait him into a big exchange. The strategy must have worked because Vovchanchyn came at me with a big overhand left, followed by a right that stunned me and backed me into a corner. On the ropes, Vovchanchyn attacked me with some head and body shots, but I was able to withstand his barrage and get out of the corner. When he came at me again, I closed the gap and tied him up with underhooks in order to recover for a bit. I pushed him into the corner and took him down, ending up on top in his guard. From the top, I managed to get his right hand trapped underneath him and started dropping bombs on his face. When Vovchanchyn punched me from the bottom, I just smiled at him like I had done in my fight against Amir Rahnavardi.

After damaging him on the ground for a while, I let Vovchanchyn back up and tried to finish him on the feet. He kind of lunged forward to try and make up for his reach disadvantage, putting everything he had into each of his punches. I hit him with a big left hand that rocked him, but he quickly answered back with a combination to the back of my head that sent me stumbling away. As I was trying to gather myself, I slipped on the mat and hit the ground. Immediately, Vovchanchyn saw his chance and jumped on me, hitting me with some big punches that caused the referee to stop the fight. I put my hands up in protest, but it didn't matter because the fight was over. I tried the best that I could against him, but it just wasn't good enough at the time. The same thing that happened in our first fight happened again in our second: Vovchanchyn saw an opening and took it.

After a tough fight against me that lasted 10 minutes, Vovchanchyn still had to fight two more times that night. He faced Kazushi Sakuraba in a 15-minute war, before eventually losing in the finals to my friend Mark Coleman, who became the first Pride Grand Prix tournament winner.

I was disappointed that I had lost twice to Vovchanchyn, but there was no shame in doing so. He hits like a jackhammer, meaning he's accurate, powerful, and by far the best striker I've ever faced in mixed martial arts. Vovchanchyn's the hardest hitter in the sport, and when he connects, you're pretty much done. Anyone who beat him standing just got lucky. We became fast friends after our fights, because we're both warriors cut from the same cloth. We're friends outside of the ring, but inside, we go to war.

My first fight against Vovchanchyn was also significant because it was the fight at which I met my second wife, Karen Elizabeth Goodridge II, also known as "White Karen." Karen and I had been carrying on an internet relationship for quite some time before she came to the fight. We had first started talking when I was still with Charlie Austin, Trinity's mother. Even though I was living with Charlie and we were having a baby together, in reality, we were done. When Karen and I started off, we were just good friends online and on the phone. Eventually our relationship began to occupy all of my time, so I turned my full attention toward it. I was falling in love with another woman, and it was intriguing for me because I'd never been in a relationship with somebody on the internet before.

Karen was born in Nova Scotia, but since her dad was in the Canadian Air Force, her family had moved around a lot. For a while Karen lived in France until her father was transferred to Germany, where they ended up in a tent city. At the age of 13, Karen returned to Canada and settled at Base Borden near Barrie. She went to the University of Alberta in Edmonton and when she returned to Barrie, she started her own family law practice. Now she works as the senior legal counsel at the Children's Aid Society for Simcoe County. Obviously, Karen is extremely intelligent, which was very attractive to me.

Karen and I had been chatting online for several months before the Vovchanchyn fight. We would also talk on the phone for hours on end, just getting to know each other. I really wanted to see Karen, so I asked her if she would come to Japan to watch one of my fights. I was somewhat surprised when Karen actually agreed to come, but it was definitely a good surprise. I told Karen that we would be sharing a room and that I hoped it wasn't a problem. Karen always had a great sense of humor, and I laughed when she assured me she was a big girl and could handle herself. Karen was smart about it: coming to Japan would be a strange situation, since we had never met before. She had to trust somebody whom she had never even met, in a country she had no familiarity with. Clearly, there were a lot of trust issues, but she covered as many bases as possible. She knew my sister Susie attended most of my fights, and she wanted to make sure she was going to be at that particular fight. Before she went to Japan, Karen asked for my sister's phone number and called her. Being the great sister that she is, Susie said, "Of course you can come. No problem. If you're a friend of Gary's, you can bunk with me."

When I met Karen, she was a complete lady from the first moment. While we were chatting, getting to know each other, she used to talk about how much she ran and I wanted to see her legs. I asked her to wear a mini-skirt when we met. It was a challenge that I put out for her, and she accepted. When Karen walked into the lobby of the Tokyo Hilton, she was wearing a grey sweater and a pink mini-skirt that absolutely impressed the hell out of me. That night Susie got a room with two beds and Karen stayed with her. I had my own king-size bed and thought to myself, *We'll see how long this lasts.* It wasn't a big surprise when a couple of nights later, she ended up in my hotel room. We had a great time together. From that point on, we were off to the races, and it wasn't long before I fell completely in love with her. Until I met Karen, I had never truly fallen in love. Prior to that, the only love that I had really felt that would be comparable was the love I felt for my daughter Trinity. Karen is a quiet soul. She never says too much about anything. I still don't even know whether or not she liked the fact that I was a fighter. I mean, she must have liked *something* about it, but I never heard what because she keeps most things to herself.

Karen and I never got divorced, but we've been separated since December 2004. Eventually, she got sick of the fact that I cannot be monogamous. As much as I try to fake it for a while, I am not a monogamous creature. After she left, I really wanted her back, but it never happened. Even now, it's been years since we separated and I still love that woman to death. There is nothing in the world I wouldn't do for her. She's got me for life. It is a credit to both of our characters and personalities that we've been able to stay friends since then. We are both pretty calm people, and we stay focused on what our daughter Tyra needs. We've never once had a disagreement about anything when it comes to Tyra. If somebody has family coming in from out of town and one of us needs to take Tyra for a couple extra days, it is no big deal.

I went into the relationship with Karen with the best intentions. We both thought we would grow old together, but things didn't work out like that for a lot of reasons that are very personal. What I can say is that the lifestyle of a professional athlete is probably an issue a lot of couples have to deal with. Karen saw the way women were just throwing themselves at me and she would have needed some sort of superhuman resolve to just ignore it. She hasn't really dated since we broke up, because she has just been focused on work and Tyra. She did date for a couple of years, but I think that potential new boyfriends find me a pretty intimidating ex, even though I've tried not to be the jealous type.

From left, Shirma, my mother, Sharon, Lisa, and Susie lifting me up at my 40th birthday party. My sisters and I have a pact that we all have to travel to celebrate each sibling's 40th birthday all together.

(*below*) Just another day at the Uptown Boxing Gym in Barrie. My daughter Tyra is about nine months old in this picture.

Another shot at the local boxing club. I wanted a photo-shoot with the rustic old gym behind me. Trinity is on the floor and Tyra is on my shoulder.

This is the classic beefcake shot. I got the Superman tattoo before my first UFC fight.

This is me sporting the flag of my birth country, Trinidad and Tobago. The towel around my neck was just a habit I got into — to soak up the sweat and to help hold my neck up straight. Tom Erikson used to do it for me. Before you fight, all of your muscles need to be warmed up. Boxers don't wear a gown because they're showing off; they do it to stay warm before they fight.

Here I am arm-wrestling Kevin Kelly, from Kitchener. I'm in my early 20s, and you can see I still have hair in this picture. This shot was taken as I was jumping into a shoulder roll, on my way to pinning Kelly.

(below) My second fight against Igor Vovchanchyn. The picture was taken right before he knocked me senseless and I stumbled across the ring. Igor is very deceiving; he looks like nothing but he packs a hard punch. We fought twice and both times he had my number.

Mike Mobbs took this picture after my last boxing fight against David Bostice. I'm about 27 years old, and it was the first time I ever got a black eye and a concussion.

This is me trying to look as menacing as possible and showing off my right bicep, my main attribute in arm-wrestling and fighting.

Right after I knocked out Sylvester Terkay, I jumped on the ropes for my signature celebration. It was always my favorite part of a fight. ▶

◀ Susie and I going out for a K-1 fight. She's pumping up the crowd, and people loved to see her in my corner. I always celebrated before I fought, which is why the Japanese crowds loved me. I always brought excitement.

Here I am at a studio in Toronto, wearing a pair of gloves from Pride FC. Before I competed in Japan, I had the Japanese characters "Go-Riki" tattooed on my left bicep. That translates to "superhuman strength" or "maximum power."

Here I am about to knock out Carter Williams. He blocked the punch with his left but his other hand was at his waist and I was lined up for a left.

CHAPTER **NINE**

I may not have won the Pride Grand Prix 2000, but there was still a home for me with the organization since the Japanese public continued to enjoy my fighting style. It was always all or nothing with me and I never gave up, just like a samurai. Pride always concentrated on the character fighters brought into the ring, so they wanted to give me some kind of title. Pride loved Bob Sapp and his "Beast" character. Sapp, a former NFL player who got into fighting, was extremely successful in Japan, appearing in many television shows and commercials. I love Bob Sapp. He came out and made a lot of money from theatrics and his enormous size. He's a really good actor, and his strength and his size make him very difficult to deal with. As a fighter, Sapp learned a lot from Josh Barnett and was a training partner of Josh's for many, many years. He's not as foolish as the character he plays; he's actually very knowledgeable and he can kick ass. I always look forward to his fights. Sapp knows how to move, trust me. He doesn't like getting punched at all, but if his opponents can't knock him out, their wrestling isn't going to do anything because Sapp just powers through it.

I was good enough that I wasn't losing all of the time, but I wasn't great enough to win their heavyweight championship, so Pride decided to nickname me the "Gatekeeper." If Pride wanted to call me that, it was fine. It didn't mean anything to me, but at least it paid the bills. As the "Gatekeeper," I controlled the access other fighters had to Pride. If a fighter could beat me, they were allowed into Pride. If they couldn't beat me, Pride didn't want them. After the Pride Grand Prix 2000, I really did live up to my nickname by beating up all of the top up-and-coming fighters except for the heavyweights who were on their way to becoming the elite fighters in the world.

• • •

At Pride 9: New Blood in June 2000, which took place at the Nagoya Rainbow Hall in Nagoya, Japan, I competed against Ricco Rodriguez. Ricco was a tough fighter who would later go on to win the UFC heavyweight title against Randy Couture. However, when we met, Ricco Rodriguez was still relatively unknown and making his debut appearance in Pride after winning the King of the Cage heavyweight championship. When Ricco entered mixed martial arts, he did so as an accomplished wrestler and Brazilian Jiu-jitsu practitioner. Ricco proved his mettle in both of those disciplines by winning a gold medal at the prestigious Abu Dhabi Combat Club Submission Wrestling World Championship in 1998. Ricco had also started training in Phoenix with top fighters like Bas Rutten and Mark Kerr and had been working on his Thai boxing. Needless to say, I thought Ricco was pretty tough going into the fight.

The early part of the fight consisted of me trying to keep the fight standing by stuffing all of his takedown attempts. After stuffing three attempts in a row, Ricco finally managed to take me down. On the ground, Ricco struggled for a while to pass my guard but couldn't. While we were hitting each other with punches on the ground, he gave me a shot to the groin, making me wince in pain. Right away, Ricco looked to the referee and said, "Come on!" as if he thought I was faking. He ended up getting a caution from the referee; it took me a few minutes to shake off the pain. I couldn't help but be relieved I was wearing my new steel cup and I didn't have to worry about my jock caving in again. After the fight started again, Ricco shot for a take-down, but I sprawled and hit him with a big right hand that hurt him. I started loading up my right after that, showing him I could hit him with it again. When we clinched, I went for a standing guillotine choke, which gave him the opportunity to get me down. Once on the ground, he was able to transition from side mount to full mount. Fortunately, there was only a minute left in the first round and I was able to keep Ricco wrapped up until the bell rang.

Round two played out much like the first. I hit Ricco with a big right hand early and was able to stuff his takedown once, but eventually he grabbed a hold of a single leg and took me to the ground. From half-guard, Ricco cross-faced me and hit me with a few body shots. Then, for some reason, he started hitting me with palm strikes to the side of my head that didn't do anything at all. Realizing this, he went for a leg lock. As soon as he attempted it, I countered by grabbing his leg and threatening a submission of my own. Ricco gave up on my leg and managed to get the full mount on me again. However, he couldn't do anything with his superior position. He attempted a few more sub-missions but I easily defended them all and Ricco just held me down until the fight ended. Ricco had won the fight on the scorecards, but for a highly touted submission grappler, he was never once close to ending the fight.

Due to the fact that he was a former UFC champ, a lot of fight fans give Ricco Rodriguez more credit than he's ever deserved. Sure, he's good at submissions, but I knew absolutely nothing about submissions and I went the distance with him. What does that tell you? I didn't even know how to apply an arm bar, let alone defend one, and yet he couldn't submit me. That just tells you where Ricco's level was at. Maybe I'm not giving him enough credit because he might have been worried too much about my strikes, but Ricco was clearly not a top submission heavyweight like Antonio Rodrigo Nogueira.

I mentioned before how many top-ranked fighters were the type of fighter who was afraid to take certain fights. Ricco Rodriguez is another fighter who won't take a fight unless he's confident that he can win. That kind of attitude is something I really don't like. Ricco has had so many chances to do well in this business, but he's just pissed on everyone and burned all of his bridges. He can be a hell of a nice fighter, and he acts pretty cool around other fighters when he actually does fight. The problem is, he needs things set up properly, and that's got coward written all over it. He's too stuck on looking good. He claims he wants to fight everybody, but in reality, he doesn't want to fight anybody he thinks might beat him.

• • •

Following my decision loss to Ricco Rodriguez, I faced off against Gilbert "The Hurricane" Yvel in front of 35,000 people at Pride 10: Return of the Warriors in August 2000. Gilbert Yvel is a Dutch Muay Thai fighter who earned a reputation as a tough son of a bitch with the Rings organization before entering Pride. When I fought Gilbert Yvel, I went out there and thought I was going to beat him. The game plan was to take him down to the ground because I knew that Yvel was a dangerous stand-up fighter and I didn't want to stand with him. Of course, I'm also known as a stand-up fighter, but I wanted to make the fight easier on myself by taking him to the ground because I figured that I knew more about grappling than Yvel.

At the start of the fight, Yvel and I squared off and were watching each other closely, trying to fake each other out. I knew Yvel was skilled at Muay Thai so when I saw him throw a kick, I thought, *Okay, it's coming to my leg.* By the time I realized the kick was actually coming to my head, it was too late. His kick caught me in the head and knocked me out just 28 seconds into the fight. I don't remember anything about the knockout — I pretty much only woke up when I was in the changing room backstage. Obviously, I woke up and walked out of the ring, but I really wasn't conscious until I was in the back. After the knockout, I could vividly remember little bits, but I couldn't remember everything. Mostly the experience is a blur — I was that messed up.

My fight with Yvel was the first time in my life I had ever been knocked out. As soon as the fight was over, I was put in an ambulance and sent to the hospital. Every time a fighter got knocked out, Pride would send them to a hospital to get a CAT scan. They needed to make sure the brain's functioning properly and the blood is flowing right. All the same, getting knocked out is really no big deal, and I have no hard feelings toward Yvel. In fact, he's one of my favorite fighters to watch, along with Wanderlei Silva, Quinton "Rampage" Jackson, Tank Abbott, and Phil Baroni. All of those fighters are characters who create excitement, which is exactly the type of fighter I am. As far as his reputation goes, if there was ever a dirty fighter, it is Gilbert Yvel. Yvel earned that reputation by repeatedly and deliberately poking people in the eyes, which he famously did against Don Frye. Yvel also punched out a referee once in the middle of the fight. Despite Yvel's reputation, in person he's a good kid, if a little high-strung.

The quick string of three wins I had over tough competition following the Yvel fight is proof the knockout didn't have any affect on my mental game. At Pride 11: Battle of the Rising Sun in Osaka, Japan, I defeated Yoshiaki Yatsu. Yatsu, a Japanese professional wrestler, was making his greatly hyped mixed martial arts debut. He may not have had any mixed martial arts experience, but he had good wrestling skills, having competed in the 1976 Montreal Olympics. In pro wrestling, Yatsu made his name with the All Japan Pro Wrestling organization and was even known in North America after challenging WWF world heavyweight champion Hulk Hogan to a match.

From the opening bell, I gave Yatsu a big beating, hitting him with a ton of hard leg kicks and big uppercuts. Every time he failed a takedown, I'd make him pay for it by pummeling him with more punches. After a while, I was surprised he hadn't yet been knocked out, and when the crowd started chanting his name, I realized I needed to pace myself. I was able to hit him at will, but if he wasn't going to drop easily, I needed to conserve energy. I kept hitting Yatsu with hard low kicks while he kept trying desperately to take me down. Whenever he would go for a single leg, I would stuff the takedown and hit him with huge uppercuts that landed flush on his chin.

Yatsu just wouldn't fall, so when he went for a single leg again, I jumped guard and tried to finish him with a guillotine choke. When he escaped, he went for a leg lock, but even though it hurt a bit, he had nothing. I escaped the leg lock and managed to take Yatsu's back and nail him with some hard shots. As I was attempting to get the fight standing again, I saw he was vulnerable for a knee to the head that could end the fight. Unfortunately, Yatsu was still on the ground, so my knee strike was illegal in Pride at the time. As a result, I received a yellow card, docking me 10 percent of my fight purse. Since Yatsu was all right, the fight resumed, and I attacked him with massive uppercuts that rocked his head back violently. Unbelievably, Yatsu never once fell down. Eventually the referee had seen enough damage and stepped in to stop the fight.

One thing that I can say about Yatsu is that he is a guy who can take a beating. He's like a Timex watch. I don't think I could ever take a beating like that guy did, though he was never much of a mixed martial artist.

After the fight with Yatsu, I started doing a few things differently in my training regimen. Instead of my normal training of running up hills to work on my cardio, I focused more on mixed martial arts–based cardiovascular training. Fight-specific training would hopefully step up my overall game. Along with getting back to lifting weights, I got cardio training by grappling and doing target mitt and sparring sessions.

I next competed outside of Pride at an event called 2 Hot 2 Handle, a promotion based out of Rotterdam, Netherlands. At 2 Hot 2 Handle, I fought "Dirty" Bob Schrijber and ended up with a knee bar submission win a couple minutes into the first round. As far as I'm concerned, I should not have won that fight. Schrijber was a better striker than me and he did everything he could to keep my head out of the game. He had me beat, but I ended up pulling a submission win out of my ass. That had never happened before in my career and it never happened again.

I returned to the Pride ring to fight Valentijn "The Python" Overeem at Pride 14 in Yokohama, Japan. Valentijn is the brother of Alistair Overeem, another popular fighter. The Overeem brothers are both great stand-up fighters from Holland, and Valentijn had a lot of experience. In the Rings organization, he had already achieved big wins over Randy Couture and Renato "Babalu" Sobral. I knew that Overeem was going to be tough; I also knew he was somebody I needed to beat if I wanted to keep on getting work.

At the beginning of our fight, Overeem came out with some low kicks and then shot in for a takedown. After stuffing the takedown, I hit him with some big knees and decided to take him down. From the bottom, he went for some submissions but I was too strong for him and I kept yanking my arm out. On the ground, I hit him with a big left knee that rocked him pretty damn hard. As he tried to cover up, I hit him with a number of punches and he tapped out.

After my three-fight win streak against Yatsu, Schrijber, and Overeem, I competed against Antonio Rodrigo "Minotauro" Nogueira at Pride 15. Nogueira was making his Pride debut after developing a reputation as a dangerous Brazilian Jiu-jitsu fighter with the Rings promotion. At 6'3" and a very lean 240 pounds, Nogueira is about as tough a fighter as you'll ever find. At the age of 10, Nogueira was run over by a truck, putting him in a four-day coma and in the hospital for a year. Nogueira had a miraculous recovery, and the kind of toughness he developed from the accident helped him keep his cool whenever he got into a bad situation during fights. Originally, I wasn't even supposed to be fighting at Pride 15. I took that fight on a week's notice after Mark Coleman hurt his knee in training and had to pull out. When Pride called and asked me to take the fight, I was already in Japan — I had to fly home first to take care of some things before turning right around and flying back for the event. It wasn't the most ideal situation, but I never turn down a challenge.

Throughout the entire fight against Nogueira, I was in defensive mode, just trying to protect myself from his submission attempts. When the first round started, Nogueira went for a takedown and I sprawled and let him back up. After stuffing his takedown a second time, he pulled guard. From there, he swept me and maneuvered into my half-guard. When I scrambled, I ended up on top again and started hitting him with some hard punches. However, in the midst of pounding on him, he got sneaky and managed to catch me in a triangle choke, forcing me to tap out.

The Nogueira fight was the first time that I had ever been finished with a triangle choke. After that, I decided to practice triangle chokes a lot. Anytime somebody takes me out in a new way, I practice that move a lot because I want to take somebody else out in the same way. After Yvel kicked me in the head, for example, I decided I was not going to leave mixed martial arts until I knocked somebody out with a head kick. I was determined to do it and, of course, that's what ended up happening in my "retirement" fight against Don Frye. I always really wanted to catch somebody in a triangle choke the same way Nogueira beat me, but it hasn't happened.

Once Nogueira got by me, he went on a tear through the heavyweight division in Pride, losing only three times: once in a controversial decision loss to Josh Barnett, the other two at the hands of Fedor Emelianenko. The list of fighters Nogueira has defeated throughout his career is pretty incredible. On his way to holding the Pride and later the UFC heavyweight titles, Nogueira beat Mark Coleman, Heath Herring, Bob Sapp, Semmy Schilt, Dan Henderson, Ricco Rodriguez, Mirko "Cro Cop" Filipovic, Tim Sylvia, and (in a rematch) Josh Barnett. He earned his reputation as an incredible fighter due to his ability to pull out a submission win at any time. He has the tools to beat any other fighter because he's got the best submissions in the heavyweight division. Since our fight, I've gotten to know him and I have to say he's just an all-around good guy. I've been out at the clubs dancing with him and we've become friends because he always speaks from his heart, which is something I really respect.

The loss to Nogueira didn't affect me at all and it wasn't long before I pulled together another string of quality wins. At the K-1 Andy Memorial 2001 Japan Grand Prix Final, I defeated Jan Nortje with an arm bar submission only one minute and 11 seconds into the first round. Jan Nortje is a 6'10", 330-pound giant; more importantly, he is a really good friend of mine. On the first punch Nortje threw, he hit me square in the eye, and it closed up immediately. After that, all I could do was reach out and grab him. When he pushed back against me, he ended up pulling himself into the corner, which is exactly where I wanted him. In the corner I used a leg trip to get him down to the ground and then hit him with a barrage of hard punches. Nortje shielded himself from the assault by stretching his arms out, which gave me the opening for an arm bar, so I took it and finished him with a quick submission.

Following my win over Nortje, I competed at Pride 16 in a rematch against Yoshiaki Yatsu, who had taken an incredible beating from me less than a year earlier. Apparently he had been working on his boxing and sambo, but it didn't make much of a difference. It was only Yatsu's second mixed martial arts fight and it would prove to be his last: I gave him another classic beat-down. All of the cardio-based changes I had made to my training regimen paid off, and I beat Yatsu more quickly the second time than the first. In our second fight, Yatsu kept attempting to take me down, but I kept stuffing his shots and making him pay for it every time with knees and punches. I kept nailing him with my jab and punishing him with uppercuts every time he tried to clinch with me. After watching their fighter take three minutes of non-stop punishment, Yatsu's corner threw in the towel.

• • •

Following my second win over Yatsu, I had a grueling five-round draw against the Brazilian Ebenezer Fontes Braga on New Year's Eve, at Inoki Bom-Ba-Ye 2001. My wife was heavily pregnant with my second daughter, Tyra, at the time. I had missed the birth of my first daughter, Trinity, because of a fight, and there was no way I was going to miss my second daughter's birth. Luckily the timing worked out with Tyra.

I had worn Karen down when it came to convincing her to have another kid. She had three older kids, who are now in their 20s, so she was done having kids. The problem was I had always wanted another child to go along with Trinity. So I worked on convincing her for a year before she agreed and we finally decided to have Tyra.

On January 24, 2002, I was lying in bed with Karen and Trinity when Karen had a contraction. At first, Karen and I just shrugged it off because she had felt contractions a few days prior but nothing had happened. However, a few minutes later, she suddenly got up and held onto the dresser. When she got another contraction and bent over in pain, I thought it was really funny. Since I knew that she would be all right, I was just making fun of her. I even went and got the camera so that I could take a picture of her bent over in pain. After a few contractions, Trinity, who was by now two years old, started to get excited. She knew she was about to have a sister, so she jumped up and started screaming at me, "Baby! Baby, Daddy, baby!"

Trinity may have been excited, but I wasn't, at least not at first. It was late at night and I just wanted to go to sleep. I didn't want to go to the hospital again for another false alarm. However, because I didn't want to be an uncaring husband, I got ready to go. In my defense, Karen also figured she wasn't really going into labor, so we were just taking our time, getting dressed and packing our bags to go to the hospital. As we were making sure we had everything, Karen's contractions quickened. It wasn't long before we both realized this could be the real thing. That's when I started to get really excited. By the time we got everything packed into the car, there was no doubt she was about to have our baby, so I drove as fast as I could to get to the Royal Victoria Hospital in Barrie.

One of the great things about Karen has always been her sense of humor. Even when she was in the tremendous pain of labor, Karen still managed to make fun of me the entire way to the hospital. A few days earlier, we had gone to the hospital for one of her false alarms. While we were there, some police officers pulled her aside and asked if I was beating her. Karen was incredulous. "No, of course not!" she told them. "He's my husband!" To this day, I still don't know what those idiot cops thought they saw, but I wasn't too happy about it. The night Karen and I were on the way to the hospital for the real thing, she joked the whole time that the police would be ready and waiting to arrest me when we got there. I have to admit, it was pretty funny.

Once we got to the hospital and checked in, a nurse took Karen into one of the rooms and hooked her up to all sorts of monitors. Let me tell you, it was weird. First, they stripped her down to just a gown and then had to spread her legs while everybody crowded around to see what was inside. I don't know how women can go through that. Before she went into labor, Karen and I talked about it and she had decided she didn't want to take any kind of drugs during the delivery. She had birthed three children before and had never needed any drugs. However, about six hours into the delivery of Tyra, she changed her mind and started begging for an epidural! "I don't want to feel any-thing," she pleaded, "I want to go to sleep." I certainly wasn't going to argue, so I helped hold Karen up while the doctor washed her back and put the needle in her spine. The next thing you know, Karen was still having contractions but she couldn't feel any pain, just the move-ments. Not long after that, Tyra was born. I even got to cut the umbil-ical cord, which was an amazing experience. Finally, I had seen one of my babies being born. It was a completely overwhelming feeling and I broke down into tears right there in the hospital. It was the greatest moment I have ever experienced in my life.

· · ·

I spent a few months after Tyra was born just hanging out with my kids, enjoying family life and giving some nagging injuries time to heal. However, as a fighter, I was feeling the urge to compete again and to make some money, so it wasn't long before I was back in the gym preparing to fight. During the summer of 2002, I got back into the ring at Pride 21 against Achmed Labasanov. Labasanov was 12 years younger than me and had trained with the Russian Top Team. It was his first fight in Pride, and I was ready to have a big comeback and kick his ass.

I knew Labasanov was good on the ground, so during my training camp for the fight, I spent a lot of time on takedown defense with Tom Erikson at Purdue University. As a wrestling coach, Tom has the keys to the Purdue athletic center, so when we go there we get to use whatever we want — the weight room, the mats, the cardio room, and, most importantly, the rehab room. As usual, I was looking to keep the fight standing and knock Labasanov out, so I also did a lot of work with Paul Minhas at Ultimate Thai Boxing in Toronto.

During the fight, Labasanov exchanged with me on our feet for a bit but quickly realized he didn't want to play that game. He threw some wild punches when we clinched and managed to sweep me off my feet and take me down. After getting half-guard, he stepped over top of me and went for an Achilles heel lock. Since I had dealt with leg locks many times before, I saw it coming and readjusted, ending up on top of him. While on top, I went for a couple of submissions, like a neck crank and a forearm choke. Unable to secure those, I punished him with some hard knees to body and head. Moving to the north-south position, I hit him with some hard knees directly to the top of his head and then moved back into side control for some more knees to the body. Eventually, he scrambled and managed to end up on top in my closed guard. However, he didn't have much of a chance to do anything because the round ended.

At the start of the second round, Labasanov looked beaten up, and

I wanted to finish him quickly. I came out with a high roundhouse kick that missed, so I circled and kept hitting him with low kicks. When I threw a big right hand, Labasanov changed levels and took me down. He was in my guard but not doing anything — the referee warned him he needed to work or else the fight would be stood up. He started getting busier, but his punches weren't doing anything so I held out my arms and yelled, "Woo!" As he continued to hit me, I yelled, "Come on hit me. Woo! You've got nothing." At the end of the second round, I stood up and walked around with lots of energy while Labasanov sat in his corner looking exhausted. As his corner was toweling him off, I jumped out into the middle of the ring and started bouncing around to show him I was ready to go.

When the bell rang for the start of the third round, I threw a couple of hard punches, but Labasanov managed to get another takedown. I knew I didn't want to spend the whole round on the bottom, so I rolled over onto my knees and just stood up. He couldn't get me down so I ended up on top and then hit him with some hard knees and hammer fists, which forced him to scramble to his feet. He was bleeding pretty bad and had a big mouse over his eye. Clearly, he didn't want to trade on the feet so he clinched, got double underhooks, and took me down. Once again, he wasn't able to do anything with his top position and the final round expired with him just lying on top of me.

As soon as the fight ended, Labasanov lay on the mat for a few seconds while I walked around the ring with my arms in the air. If a fight goes to a decision you have to show the judges who is in better condition after the fight. The first judge scored for Labasanov, while the second and third judges scored the fight for me. It was a split decision win for me. Pride judges decide fights based on who was closest to finishing the other guy, and I was never in danger at any point. When the verdict was announced, I threw my hands in the air in celebration. I had been inactive for a while and it felt great to get another win and kick another fighter's ass right back to the minor leagues.

After defeating Labasanov, I fought at Pride Shockwave, a

co-production between Pride and K-1, a prominent kickboxing organization in Japan that would later have a huge role in my career. Pride Shockwave was a monumental event with over 91,000 people jammed into the Tokyo National Stadium. The event ended up setting an attendance record for a mixed martial arts event. Originally, I wasn't even scheduled to compete, but I agreed to fight on short notice when another fighter dropped out. At Pride Shockwave, I faced off against Lloyd van Dams, a Muay Thai fighter from Holland who has huge, powerful legs and kicks like a mule.

Going into the fight, my plan was to test van Dams on his feet for a bit and then beat him on the ground. Once I got in there, however, I decided not to waste any time and took him down. Immediately, I got a body lock with double underhooks on him. With my underhooks in place, I pushed him up against the ropes, picked him up, and slammed him down to the ground hard. I held him down and hit him with some hard shots that made him start to bleed from his nose. For some reason, van Dams tried to fishhook me, which is illegal, so I started screaming at the referee. He stopped what he was doing, but it was too late because I was already pissed off. I quickly mounted him, held him down by his throat, and rained down huge punches. The referee had seen enough ground and pound and stopped the fight, giving me a quick victory. I hadn't taken any strikes during the fight and I had put on a much more impressive performance than I had against Labasanov. Pride executives Takada and Ishizaka came into the ring after the fight to congratulate me; it felt good to know that once again my career with Pride was secure.

CHAPTER TEN

Outside of the ring, most fighters generally have a good time together. However, conflicts and beefs occasionally happen. In order to prevent any trouble, Pride officials would separate the shuttle buses to the events into corners A and B, so that you'd never be on the same bus with somebody you were fighting against. And, if Pride already knew that two fighters didn't get along, they would also separate them, regardless of their corner.

The Brazilian fighters, in particular, would often have problems with other fight camps and probably gave the Pride officials a lot of headaches. Fighting is just how the Brazilians handle any kind of confrontation. Brazilians are so hot-blooded — they always want to fight. On the drop of a dime, they will go from being really calm and cool to an all-out massive brawl where they want to kill each other.

I remember at one point, the guys from the renowned Chute Boxe Academy out of Curitiba, Brazil, had some kind of issue with Wallid Ismail, a Brazilian fighter known for being one of the ugliest fighters around. Ismail was a black belt in Brazilian Jiu-jitsu under the famous Carlson Gracie. For some reason, Ismail wasn't getting along with one of the Gracies. I'm sure part of the problem was that Ismail had beaten four of the Gracies in jiu-jitsu tournaments, including a big win over Royce Gracie. Things eventually got so bad that Pride had to put Wallid Ismail and the Chute Boxe Academy in separate hotels.

One member of the Chute Boxe Academy who has a reputation as being particularly hotheaded is Wanderlei "The Axe-Murderer" Silva. Silva is a loose cannon just like Ken Shamrock. One minute, those guys will be talking to you calmly, the next, they'll be screaming their heads off at you and ready to fight. They're both very nice guys if you keep the conversation where they want it. However, if you don't, they go crazy. Silva is the only angry person I've ever really met in the fight game. I have seen Silva on television recently and he always looks so friendly, kissing babies and smiling. Everybody loves him now, but that's not the guy that I knew.

There were many times when Silva would just fly off the handle. I used to see Wanderlei around at the Brazilian shows before anybody in the mixed martial arts scene even knew who he was, and he was always a very aggressive individual, somebody you didn't want to mess with. He's probably grown up a little bit since then, but he's still a different breed. I always think of Brazilians as being the pit bull race of people. No disrespect to them at all — they're very aggressive and very hot-tempered, but they are also very loyal and good people.

I remember one time I was at an airport in Japan with all of the other Pride fighters, getting ready to fly from Tokyo to Saitama for Pride 19: Bad Blood. As I was sitting in the waiting area with Tom Erikson, a fight broke out between Silva and another Pride fighter in the same 205-pound weight class named Alex Stiebling. Out of nowhere, Silva started going crazy, getting right in Stiebling's face and saying, "Why you looking at me? You wanna fight? You wanna fight?" There we were, a huge group of professional fighters, including Ken Shamrock, Don Frye, and Antonio Rodrigo Nogueira, and there is an intense melee in the middle of the airport. In order to try and help, Tom Erikson and I pulled Silva aside and asked him what happened. It turned out he was pissed off because Stiebling had been looking at him too much. Obviously Stiebling wasn't trying to start a fight with Silva because that would have just been stupid. At that point, Silva was the Pride Middleweight Champion. He was on an eight-fight winning streak against some top competition and knocking everybody out in a bad way. He would later extend his streak to an unbelievable 18 wins and he also won the Pride World Grand Prix 2003 tournament.

Another time, at Pride 31: Unbreakable, Wanderlei Silva lost his temper on Mark Coleman. That night, Coleman faced Brazilian fighter Mauricio "Shogun" Rua. Only 49 seconds into the fight, Coleman went for a double leg takedown and Shogun fell awkwardly, breaking his arm — a rather ironic end to the fight, given the name chosen for the event. After Shogun broke his arm, the referee tried to step in, but Coleman pushed the referee aside and kept going after Shogun. That caused the guys in Shogun's corner, including Silva and Shogun's brother, Murilo Rua, to jump into the ring. That, in turn, prompted Coleman's corner man, Phil Baroni, to jump into the ring, and all of a sudden a huge fight broke out. In the midst of the confusion, Silva somehow fell to the ground and Coleman, who was standing over top of him, ended up stepping on his throat. The whole scene was just unbelievable.

Backstage after the fight, Coleman tried to apologize to the Chute Boxe team but Silva kept yelling, "You kick my face on the ground." Coleman later told me that he was in disbelief about the whole thing; he didn't have any bad blood with the Chute Boxe team. In fact, he and Silva were friends prior to the fight — they had appeared together in a funny Japanese commercial for Schick shaving cream. Coleman was only trying to play up the drama for the audience and make the whole incident seem bigger than it actually was (even though the feud wasn't serious, however, I know that Coleman definitely enjoyed getting to step on Silva's throat).

I've seen Silva in his share of unsanctioned fights, but it's not like I think he needs to seek professional help for his anger issues. To me, it just shows what a passionate individual "The Axe Murderer" is. It's that passion and love for exciting fights that has always made Silva one of my favorite fighters to watch. He is a very high-strung individual, driven by testosterone. He was always one of the most pumped up fighters out there.

When Silva was in Pride he was an icon. When you have people like that who are icons with an organization, they become bigger than God. An organization like Pride could not afford to have their stars look foolish, so they gave them special privileges. Guys like Silva got a ticket to do whatever it is they had to do to look good. What happened with Silva is that he bought into the hype that surrounded him. He looked so juiced up back then, but when you see him today, he is a totally different animal. The animal that fought in Pride was exactly that — an animal. The person who is fighting today is totally different, simply because of the stuff that he had been allowed to take.

I know that there was some controversy that Silva was sometimes competing heavier than he should have been. I never really got to see what was going on with other people weighing in, but in Japan if Silva was grossly overweight at 210 or 212 pounds, Pride would have allowed him to fight in the 205-pound weight class because of his position. I'm sure that happened more times than once. However, it's not really a big deal to me because in my opinion, there shouldn't be a weight class for the big boys, anyway. I think if you're over 200 pounds, you're over. It shouldn't matter whether you're 205 or 405 — either way you're over.

In North America, there are strict drug laws, but they aren't as stringent in Japan. Pride didn't give a shit what you did or what you were on as long as you made them look good. Japanese people are all about pride and ego; if everybody looks like they are juiced up on steroids and it makes the show look better, their opinion is *no problem, let's have it*. I don't think the Pride organization provided steroids and other drugs to the fighters, though I don't know for sure. In the U.S., they want to know what was in your stool yesterday — that's how strict it is to pass. The easiest way to pass in the U.S. is just to stay clean, which is why fighters don't look the way they used to look in Japan.

Despite some shady incidents and practices, the Pride organization was like a family. Most of the fighters had a lot of fun while we were together. It wasn't odd to have a whole bus full of fighters suddenly break out in song on the way to an event. Of course that was tame in comparison to some of the things that happened. Sometimes, the fighters were just animals. This was particularly true anytime there were a bunch of Dutch fighters on the bus, because they were always the craziest.

On one of the Pride bus rides, a number of Dutch fighters decided that they were going to have a competition about who had the biggest dick and who had the biggest balls. The biggest dick contest came down to Kevin Randleman and Gilbert Yvel. Everybody started cheering Randleman on, yelling, "Come on Randleman, let's see it. Go, go, go." Eventually, Randleman pulled out his salami, which meant it was up to Yvel to beat him. Gilbert wouldn't pull it out until it was completely erect, and I guess it was a good idea because he ended up winning the contest.

As for who had the biggest balls, that was Bas Boon.

Whenever crazy shit like that happened, I never participated. I didn't even want to watch. I mean, fighters have their girlfriends, wives, and sometimes even their mothers on the bus, and here these guys are carrying on like idiots. It's sort of disrespectful. At the same time, it was also pretty damn funny. That's the kind of thing you have to expect when you're getting on a bus with a bunch of male athletes.

• • •

My time as a fighter in Japan wasn't all about Pride. One thing that a lot of people don't know about me is that I did quite a bit of professional wrestling in Japan. I worked with the New Japan Pro-Wrestling organization, one of largest pro wrestling groups in Japan. New Japan was also popular around the world, having featured U.S. stars such as Hulk Hogan, Andre the Giant, Owen Hart, Chris Benoit, and Kurt Angle.

Working with New Japan Pro-Wrestling was a lot of fun. All of the fights were meant to look real, though everybody knew they weren't. When I first started with them, the organization went over various moves such as how to properly body slam somebody. The trainers also worked with me on faking punches and hammer fists. In professional wrestling, you have to hit your opponent with the palm of your hand, and then they're supposed to flutter back like they got really smashed. My sister Susie was with me during one of my training sessions and wanted to try it. It was pretty awesome to see her get to pick up this one guy who was 280 pounds and body slam him.

In my New Japan bouts, I won some fights and I lost some. Whatever the promoters said I was supposed to do, I did. Normally, wrestlers would meet with their opponent for five minutes to plan out the entire fight. Since I was so green, I had to meet with my opponents for about an hour and a half each day. We'd spend the whole time talking about and practicing the moves we were going to do. It was very important to make it look real, and I guess all of the extra practice paid off because New Japan was impressed enough with my performances that they called me back several times. I liked professional wrestling, but you can really get hurt. If you don't know how to take bumps and you're not very limber, you can get easily get injured. It's much harder on the body than mixed martial arts because it's an every night kind of thing, and that causes a lot of wear and tear on your muscles and joints.

Along with some professional wrestling, I also entered a strongman competition in Japan. The organization had asked some other fighters to take part in the competition, like Tom Erikson, Don Frye, and Mark Coleman, but they all said no. It sounded like a good challenge for me so I decided to enter. During the competition, there were a number of different strength tests that I had to compete in. In the first event, I had to compete against an opponent in a tic-tac-toe style game. I had to flip over these 250-pound logs that were black, while my Japanese opponent was trying to flip over the white logs. The object was to complete the tic-tac-toe game the fastest. There was a time limit of a minute and by the time we were done, all of the logs except for the one my opponent had just turned were my color. I just smoked him. The second and third events involved a truck pull and a sledgehammer, which I easily won, setting me up for a place in the finals.

In the finals, my opponent and I were both elevated on a platform. In between us was a Plexiglas wall about two inches thick. You could hit the wall with a sledgehammer as hard as you could and never break it. Whoever pushed the glass wall the hardest would make the other person fall off the platform. In the end, I won the contest and an SUV as a prize. Lots of the guys who were competing had arms that were bigger than my leg, but it was all about muscle endurance and cardio, two things that I had plenty of after years of training mixed martial arts.

• • •

In early 2003, I received the terrible news that my good friend Naoto Morishita had hung himself in the shower of his hotel room in Shinjuku, Tokyo. Morishita, who was 42 years old when he died, was the president of Dream Stage Entertainment, which owned Pride Fighting Championships. Morishita was the guy who had paid at least $500,000 out of his own pocket so that I could have my second wedding in a Japanese hotel. The reception was like a Pride production: Karen and I had over 500 guests at the wedding and everything about it was first class all the way. We even managed to get Quinton "Rampage" Jackson and Bas Rutten up on stage to do a rap together, congratulating us on our marriage. It was funny shit. Over the years, Morishita and I had developed an extremely strong friendship, and when I found out he had died in such a tragic way, I was devastated.

The police called his death a suicide. Morishita had only recently had a baby with his wife, a beautiful Japanese model, and he was rich and powerful. It didn't make much sense to me or to other people who knew him for Morishita to do such a thing. Due to the fact that he had supposedly been having problems with his mistress, Pride officials hinted that his domestic problems were probably the reason why he committed suicide. Since there was no proof anything else had been wrong in Morishita's life, the mainstream Japanese press ran with the suicide story. Other people weren't so sure that Morishita's love triangle was the reason that he killed himself. They pointed out that he had been under a lot of stress lately because of his job. There was a lot of pressure on him to keep making more money for Dream Stage Entertainment, especially since a number of foreign business deals he made had recently fallen through. There were also rumors that the K-1 and Pride co-promotion Pride Shockwave had cost a lot more than had been budgeted.

Some people pointed their fingers at Nobuyuki Sakakibara, the managing director of Dream Stage Entertainment. Morishita and Sakakibara were both successful businessmen who had been with Pride from the beginning, as underlings to Hiromichi Momose. Momose was Pride's financial backer who put 50 million yen into starting Dream Stage Entertainment after Pride 4. Sakakibara had commented quite a few times that Morishita was his puppet and would do anything he asked. When Morishita died, Momose seemed to fade away completely from the organization and Sakakibara became president of Pride under the financial backing of Mr. Ishizaka, known as "Mr. I." Mr. I was widely suspected of having ties to the yakuza, the powerful Japanese mob. Many people thought that even if Sakakibara had not played a direct part in Morishita's death, his yakuza connections might have had something to do with it. Regardless of what happened, the ordeal was the start of the downfall of Pride and the whole Dream Stage Entertainment organization because of the persistent rumors of the yakuza's involvement in the company.

• • •

Before Morishita died, he had issued a press release announcing the Pride Grand Prix 2003 tournament for middleweights. The card was similar to the heavyweight tournament I had been a part of in 2000, except this time, the top middleweights, including Chuck Liddell, Quinton Jackson, Wanderlei Silva, and Kazushi Sakuraba, would be fighting to determine the world champion. Along with the middleweight bouts, Pride wanted to have a few heavyweight exhibition matches. I got a call wanting to know if I would fight the Pride heavyweight champion, Fedor Emelianenko.

At 5'11", 230 pounds, the Russian Top Team–trained Fedor is a little short for a heavyweight and he looks like he doesn't have an ounce of muscle on his body. Despite his unassuming demeanor, Fedor is one of the greatest mixed martial artists of all time. Fedor was a multiple-time Russian and European combat sambo champion, and when we fought, he had recently been crowned the world sambo champ. He was also a national judo champion and had won tournaments with the prestigious Rings organization. Many MMA insiders considered Fedor the top fighter in the world. His only loss had come early in his career from an illegal elbow strike that opened up a cut and caused the fight to be stopped. Other than that one controversial loss, he had been unstoppable, beating everybody he had faced in Pride including Heath Herring, Antonio Rodrigo Nogueira twice, and the K-1 heavyweight champion Semmy Shilt.

The offer to fight Fedor Emelianenko came relatively late, but I still managed to have a proper training camp. I usually like about six to eight weeks of two-a-day workouts to train for my fights, but I still jumped at the chance despite the shorter prep time I had. I'll fight anybody, anytime, anywhere and any style; a fight with Fedor was no different. Sometimes that kind of attitude bites you in the ass, but it can also be beneficial. You have to take the chance. I didn't have as long as I would have liked to prepare for Fedor, but I spent the time I did have training hard. There was no doubt about it: a fight with Fedor was going to be tough, and I was going to have to train like mad and be on the top of my game.

When I'm in training, I try to be at the gym five days a week, as early as possible. Usually, I'll wake up at 6:30 a.m. for breakfast, and by 8 I'm in the gym doing running and weights. For cardio, I'll mostly work on sprints because you fight in sprints. After getting ridiculously tired running sprints and having an all-around serious workout, I'll shower and get out quickly so that I can spend most of the day with my family or taking care of business. In the evening, I'll sometimes work on my technique, but now that I've been fighting for so long, I don't really have to work on technique as much. For the most part, it's just the cardio I need. The number one priority going into a fight is having gas in the tank. That's why I always push myself to work really hard. When I first started out fighting, all I cared about was working on my technique. I soon realized, however, that training isn't all about technique — you have to have the cardio to go along with it.

One thing that's important to know about training is that you should never train by yourself. Anybody who says that they're training seriously alone is not. You can only push yourself so far. You need somebody to accompany you who is designated to push you and make you work. That's why I always train with other people. A lot of the time my sister Susie will train with me. If she's not around, I'll hire people to come and train with me. I'll keep a strict record of the exact length and speed of the repetitions that I'm supposed to do and I'll get my training partners to push me to achieve those goals. In order to get the most out of my workouts, I always run on a treadmill. That way everything is adjusted exactly the way I want it. I don't like running on the streets because you don't know certain things such as the incline you're on or your heart rate. Running on a treadmill is pretty hard to beat. Technology is there to break things down for us, so why not use it? During the lead-up to a fight, I used to go to Purdue University to work on takedown defense and grappling with Tom Erikson. Other times, I'd go to the Shark Tank in California. There were also a number of other fighters who would come to my house, without pay, to help me get ready, like Erikson, Mike McDonald, Maurice Smith, and Mark Coleman.

On a typical fight day, there is no training at all. I might do some small target training if there are a few things that I want to go over.

However, for the most part, I try to stay relaxed and happy. Going into a fight, you don't want any arguments or other things in your head that aren't supposed to be there. To do your job, you can't be thinking about your problems with your wife or your kids. That is why fighters never know what's going on at home when they're at training camp. The only time guys have problems in training is when they let a woman get into their head. It will take the soul out of a fighter because when you have women problems, the drive is gone. It's a deep and embedded problem that never leaves your mind, and it becomes a major obstacle for a fighter. Your mind is preoccupied with a woman when it should be occupied with knocking the shit out of the guy in front of you.

For the fight against Fedor Emelianenko, I knew I was going to need to be extremely relaxed and in control. Fedor had been rocked by a punch in his last fight against Fujita, so I wanted to keep the fight standing so that I could try and knock out the champ. Leading up to the fight, I had worked a lot on my hands with Maurice Smith and with Coleman for upper-body wrestling.

When the bell rang, Fedor immediately faked with a right followed by a big overhand left that rocked me. Sensing I was hurt, he attacked with a quick combination of punches to my face and body. After that initial onslaught, we separated for a minute, then Fedor hit me with big right and closed the distance. In the clinch, he hit me with a good knee to the body and then swept me to the ground. In my guard, Fedor waited a few seconds before posturing up and nailing me with a number of hard punches. When I covered up, Fedor got out of my guard and stood over top of me. He then unloaded with three huge soccer kicks to my head. Then Fedor jumped on me again for some ground and pound, but thankfully, the referee stopped the fight.

I never had a chance to go on the offensive against Fedor. He is a very smart fighter who uses a well thought-out strategy in each of his fights. His strategy of bum-rushing me definitely worked. During the fight, I was always on the defensive and I never had the opportunity to land a big punch and knock him out. Ironically, Fedor didn't get out of the fight without any damage: he badly injured his thumb against me and had to eventually have surgery to correct the problem.

After the loss to Fedor Emelianenko, Pride rewarded me for stepping up and taking the fight by putting me on one of their biggest cards ever. The event, Pride Final Conflict 2003, featured the last two rounds of the middleweight Grand Prix tournament and drew over 67,000 fans to the Tokyo Dome. That night I faced off against American Dan "The Bull" Bobish. Bobish is a very nice and funny guy whom I first met on one of my first trips to Brazil when I fought at the Universal Vale Tudo Fighting 6 tournament. During one of our nights out there, Bobish and Kevin Randleman, who was also fighting, invited a few friends and me to a place called Club Help.

As soon as we walked into the club, women started winking and making eyes at us. These girls were the hottest women ever, especially to me since I love Brazilian women with their big, round asses and their skinny little waists. After giving us the eye, all of these amazing women started coming up to us and we were all wondering what the hell was going on. It was like we had walked into a twilight zone or something. I started feeling like I was Sylvester Stallone or somebody else of major league importance. All of a sudden, it hit me: Club Help was a place where people went to get sexual "help." It was a whorehouse, and almost every single woman there was selling her body. A little while later, our group decided to go back to the hotel. I brought the woman I had been dancing with up to my hotel room, and we fooled around for a bit but when she started asking me for money, I cut her loose. Judging by their Vale Tudo performances the next day, it's safe to say that some of the other fighters picked up.

By the time Bobish and I fought each other at Pride Final Conflict 2003, I had figured him out and knew that he had a weak mind. Bobish is a super guy and a great person, but he was unsure about his abilities as a fighter. Fighting is in large part a mental game. In the days leading up to our fight, I tried to fuck with Bobish by showing him I was in really great shape. I made sure he saw me jumping around, doing wind sprints, and hitting the pads. He kept pretending he wasn't watching me, but I knew he was seeing it. Even when he wasn't around to see it, his corner was seeing it and letting him know I was ready to fight. I knew my games were working and that everything I was doing was going through Bobish's head when he went to bed at night. By the time we entered the ring to fight, he had already accepted a loss in his mind despite having over 30 pounds on me. Bobish can say what he wants, and I don't mean him any disrespect, but during our fight, he was looking for a warm place to land.

Before the fight against Bobish, I didn't train quite as intensely as usual because my fight against Fedor hadn't lasted very long; all of my increased training hadn't made much of a difference. In fact, it may have even been too much training, because I was feeling worn down by the time I actually got in the ring with Fedor. I wanted to be healthy and injury-free when I went up against Bobish.

Bobish started off with a weak punch and then immediately went for a takedown. When he came at me, I stayed on my "bike" and just kept moving backward, hitting him with punches as he chased after me. After hitting him with a few hard hooks and uppercuts, Bobish turned away and started pointing at his face, trying to tell the referee that my finger went in his right eye. I've replayed the fight in slow motion many times and I can't see my finger go into his eye. But let's say it did — it's a fight and shit happens. In the end, all that matters is that I got a quick win over Bobish by TKO, just 18 seconds into the fight.

CHAPTER ELEVEN

At the beginning of this book, I talked about my Pride retirement fight. The reason I was being forced to hang it up was because my ex Karen wanted full custody of my daughter Tyra, arguing that I wasn't in the country enough. Of course, when I was pressed to make a decision, I chose my daughter instead of my career. I'm not sure whether my ex expected me to choose my career over my daughter, but there wasn't ever any chance that was going to happen.

Before my retirement fight, I told my daughters I was going to quit fighting and that I would be around all the time. However, as soon as the Don Frye fight was over and it hit my ex that I would be around a lot more and making less money, she decided I didn't need to go *that* far. I guess it sunk in that instead of me paying her so much money, I wouldn't be working, and she might even have to pay *me*. And so she hit the brakes. She and her lawyers came back and said, essentially, "It's okay . . . you can fight and we'll work out all of the details. Just keep the money coming in and we'll work around everything else." I couldn't believe it!

Since I was available to fight again, when officials from K-1 (the Japanese kickboxing promotion formed by the creator of Seidokaikan karate, Kazuyoshi Ishii) called me up in late 2003 and asked me to compete for them, I agreed. I was in my late 30s, but I still felt that I had a lot of fight left in me. Besides, K-1 was offering me the same amount of money I had been making in Pride, and I couldn't turn that down. I also had some prior experience competing in K-1, which made the transition from mixed martial arts to kickboxing a little bit easier. In K-1, every fighter wore 10 oz. gloves. Similar to the Pride mixed martial arts rules, the judging was based on whether or not an effective and accurate attack was recognized and on the damages inflicted on the opponent. Like boxing, the fight was considered over if the fighter could not answer the "10 count," went down three times, or when the fighter is judged to have lost his will to continue the fight.

My earlier experience in kickboxing started in 1999 when Pride approached me about taking part in a couple of events being organized by K-1. K-1 wanted to make itself look good by beating up some well-known Pride fighters, and for whatever reason, Pride agreed. The organization had been around since the first K-1 Grand Prix in 1993, and it was world-renowned for having the best stand-up fighters in the world. The competition was so good that former U.S. kickboxing champ Maurice Smith had been knocked out by a head kick courtesy of Ernesto Hoost in the semi-finals of the first K-1 event. K-1 asked Pride if I could fight at K-1 Revenge and K-1 Spirits. Since I was under contract with Pride, when the two companies agreed to the terms, I had to go fight.

K-1 was going to be a big step up in competition from the caliber of strikers I had faced in Pride. There was really no comparison, because stand-up fighters in MMA train extensively in punching. On the other hand, K-1 fighters have the whole package. Not only do they have hand skills, they also have kicking skills. When I entered K-1, I started out at the highest level of the sport, just like everything else I've ever done in my life. In boxing, I had fought for the national title after less than a year of being in the sport. After that, I lied my way into the UFC and started off at the highest level of mixed martial arts. Going into K-1 was the same thing — right away I faced the best kickboxers in the world.

In my first kickboxing match in 1999, I faced off against Akio Mori, a famous Japanese kickboxer more commonly known as Musashi (who took his nickname from the iconic Japanese samurai Miyamoto Musashi). Musashi had burst onto the K-1 scene in 1995 when he knocked out former UFC star Patrick Smith with a head kick. By the time we fought, Musashi had racked up a lot of kickboxing experience, having been in the ring with Mike Bernardo, Andy Hug, Branko Cikatic, and Ernesto Hoost, to name just a few. Musashi was also accomplished at other stand-up disciplines and had just won the WAKO World Heavyweight Muay Thai Championship.

Musashi started off by attacking me with leg kicks. After a right low kick buckled my leg for a minute, I backed away, but he hit me with another one. I chased after Musashi, trying to land a big punch, but he literally ran around the ring to get away from me. Finally when Musashi engaged again, he hit me with a right roundhouse kick to the head, followed by another right low kick. He quickly immobilized me with leg kicks, and pretty soon I got fed up with being a sitting target for him. I didn't know how to fight his sport, and he was tearing my legs up. To try and save myself, I grabbed hold of him in a Muay Thai clinch and threw two quick knees, accidently hitting Musashi in the nuts.

Right away, Musashi fell down in excruciating pain. I hit him so hard that I must have knocked his nuts up his throat. I didn't mean to do it; I had only had a short training camp before the fight, and I didn't aim properly. Thank God Musashi had a steel jock on or he would have been coughing out his testicles. Years later, Musashi and I had a rematch, since our first clash had such a disappointing ending. He was more of a counter-striker, so I came forward the entire fight and ended up winning a five-round decision.

My fight with Musashi was the first time in my career that I had ever taken a leg kick. I went into K-1 like a bully, thinking, *Oh yeah, I can do this. I used to box.* However, that first leg kick sent shivers up my spine. Right away I thought, *Oh my God, what have I gotten myself into?* I will never forget the fear that a proper leg kick evokes. You can practice leg kicks and receive lots of them in training, but you will never be able understand the pain involved until you're in a fight and somebody gives you a good one. When Musashi hit me, it lit up my whole body and I wanted to run out of the ring — never mind thinking about hitting him back or anything else.

Since my first kickboxing fights, I've gotten better at taking leg kicks. By hitting the bag and pads you eventually grow numb to taking the shots. Your legs graduate from being baby legs to being adult legs. With a lot of work and training, you get accustomed to the kicks. You can handle the pain better. And there is an inside secret to taking leg kicks that I didn't know anything about for a long time. What you do is take some Novocain and inject it in your legs so that it freezes. That way, you can still feel the kick, but you don't feel the pain. You can sit there and take leg kicks all day. In North America, using numbing agents like that is illegal, but in Japanese fighting, everything was legal.

In my second K-1 fight, I faced off against Masaaki Satake, an early standout in Kazuyoshi's Seidokaikan organization. Like Musashi, Satake was very experienced, having been the 1993 Karate World Cup Champion and a two-time K-1 tournament champion. I didn't think Satake was as tough as Musashi, but because I was inexperienced, Satake had a big advantage over me. Satake and I were pretty even in boxing skills, but it was his low kicks that really hurt me. Every time Satake would kick me, he'd quickly back out of the way of my counters. It wasn't long before I was walking around the ring with a noticeable limp. After another big kick buckled me, I had to take a second to collect myself. Satake saw that I had been hurt and stalked me into the corner, barely missing with a left roundhouse kick. By that point, I could hardly even stand, so I had to put my knee down on the canvas for an eight count. In the third round, I had taken too much punishment to defend myself properly, and Satake knocked me out with a kick.

I didn't like kickboxing from the minute I started doing it. The leg kicks were just too painful. As soon as the Musashi and Satake fights were finished, I went backstage and couldn't stop crying. I don't even know why I was crying, because it definitely didn't make me feel any better. My legs were in so much pain, it was just all I could do. To this day, it was the worst pain I've ever felt. I got away from the sport after those first two matches, so I could concentrate exclusively on mixed martial arts.

In the summer of 2002, after a few years away from kickboxing, K-1 contacted Pride again about having me compete against some of their heavyweights; once again, Pride agreed. I had improved my stand-up skills since the fights against Musashi and Satake, but I still went into the K-1 organization relatively inexperienced. I knew that I had the strength to compete, but not the technique. As a result, I entered K-1 with a kick-ass, whirlwind style. I knew that I probably wouldn't win on the judges' scorecards, so I just jumped into all of the fights and got right into my opponents' faces. The longer I stayed in the fight, the easier it would be for my opponents to discover I didn't really know what I was doing and to figure out a way to take me apart. I have weight and size going for me, so I just forced my opponents to deal with my tenacity right away. My plan was always to kick ass and get out of there quickly.

Coming out like a whirlwind was definitely my strategy when K-1 matched me up against Mike Bernardo at the K-1 World Grand Prix 2002 in Las Vegas. During his long career in K-1 against the world's best kickboxers, South African Mike Bernardo rarely lost, and most of his wins had come by knockout. At 6'4", 230 pounds, Bernardo had an impressive resume: he was an Olympic kickboxing super heavyweight champion, a world Muay Thai champion, and he would eventually go on to become the World Boxing Federation Heavyweight Champion.

Mike Bernardo was one of best fighters in the K-1 organization. Going into our fight, I was a huge underdog. I knew he was leaps and bounds ahead of me at that point, and it was basically like he was fighting a beginner. Sure, I had a lot of experience in fighting, but I didn't have a lot of knowledge and know-how when it came to pure striking. In the days leading up to the fight, Mike Bernardo was telling the press he was 100 percent sure he was going to beat me. I was also pretty sure that he was going to beat me, but when I talked with my corner in the locker room before the fight, they reminded me that I had nothing to lose and everything to gain. We didn't think that Bernardo could handle 260 pounds coming at him full steam for three minutes, so we decided I would go from 0 to 60 in two seconds and just see what happened. I knew that I couldn't sit around and tap away with Bernardo. I didn't want to get into a drawn-out technical battle, because he would have beat me hands down. I had to bum-rush him and force him to fight me right from the beginning. That way, it became about strength and who connected first.

I went out there and right away just started throwing bombs. I was trying to keep Bernardo on his toes and backing away from the fire. Eventually, I caught him with a huge right hook that floored him. After he fell, I hit him again, forcing the referee to pull me off him. That was the difference between K-1 and Pride rules: when an opponent goes down to the mat in Pride, you jump right in and keep punching. In K-1, if your opponent is down, you have to go to your corner and wait for the referee to restart or end the fight. It was hard for me to remember I was fighting under K-1 rules. Bernardo's corner was really pissed, so I walked across the ring, touched gloves with him, and told him I was sorry; it was an honest mistake.

As soon as we restarted, I quickly went after Bernardo again, hitting him with some big rights and lefts that sent him ducking into the corner. While he was up against the ropes, I hit him with a few big overhand rights that were really hurting him. Bernardo tried to clinch and recover, but I pushed him off me and loaded up on a huge right hand that rocked him and sent him face-first into the canvas. Bernardo managed to get up during the eight count, but he wasn't fully there mentally, and the referee wouldn't let him continue. I knew that there was no way Bernardo could continue after a knockout like that, and the referee agreed. When I knocked Bernardo out, I was so excited, I put both of my arms up and did a little dance in celebration. Nobody had expected me to knock Bernardo out; I had just accomplished one of the biggest upsets in K-1 history.

After our fight, Bernardo had a personal beef with me. The loss left him humiliated and embarrassed. He knew he should not have lost to me, since I hadn't beaten anybody of note in kickboxing. A few months later, Bernardo got a rematch against me at Inoki Bom-Ba-Ye 2002 on New Year's Eve in Japan. It was a last-minute fight for both of us, but I jumped at the opportunity, because Bernardo had made things personal. During the press conference, I won the war of words, which pissed Bernardo off even more. Going into our second fight, he definitely had something to prove.

I used the same strategy as in the first. This time it didn't work, because he saw it coming. Had I done anything else, I would've lost anyway, so what was I going to do? The way I saw it, I could go in there and lose in a long and painful match, or I could push the fight and have it over quick, win or lose. I knew it was *possible* I could beat Bernardo again but not probable. When the bell rang, I came out and hit him with a flurry of punches that backed him into the corner and had him ducking and trying to get away. He tried to clinch, but I pushed him off me and hit him with a huge overhand right. Bernardo was falling forward trying to clinch again, so I stepped back, held him with my left hand, and hit him with another big right that knocked him down. The referee yelled at me to get back to my corner and wait for Bernardo to get up during the eight count. When we restarted, I charged at him again and all he could do was cover up and back away.

After surviving my initial onslaught, Bernardo started to open up on me and he hit me with some big hooks and uppercuts. When a right low kick buckled my leg, I smiled and charged at him with some big punches. We were trading huge blows when, finally, Bernardo hit me with a straight one-two combination that sent me falling face-first to the canvas in front of my corner. I got up by the eight count, shook it off, and squared off against him again. Bernardo went off on me with some big punches, some knees to the body, and more low kicks. As I came forward with a jab, I let my other hand down and got hit with another straight one-two combination that sent me to the canvas for the count.

After the knockdown, Bernardo started to walk away but then decided to turn back around. While I was still dazed, he came back, put one foot on my back, and gave a salute to the crowd. I guess he was getting even for being embarrassed in our first fight, but it still wasn't cool. Mark Coleman, who was in my corner along with Josh Barnett, immediately got in the ring and went right over to Bernardo. Coleman was pissed and rightly so; he feels that once you're down, you're down. The winner can show off all they want, but you should *never* touch a downed opponent. If I was cornering Coleman and somebody did that to him, I would have been pissed off too. In the end, Bernardo got he what deserved: a yellow card from the referee, docking 10 percent off his pay.

For about six months after our second fight, I wanted to kick Bernardo's ass. It didn't matter to me where the fight took place: as far as I was concerned, we could even do it outside of the ring, because I can fight on the ground and he can only fight standing. I got over it with time, though. Looking back on the situation with more level-headedness, I understand why Bernardo acted the way he did after our fight. By bulldozing over him and knocking him out the first time, I had humiliated him. It would have been the same if he had come over to Pride and tapped me out with an arm bar. Bernardo needed to make it personal. And no matter what happened later, I got the first win over him and that can never be taken away from me.

Since our fights, Bernardo and I have hung out and buried the hatchet. I didn't like a few of the things he did, and he can be a bit of a dick sometimes, but overall he's a really good guy. He seems like a lost soul to me. In one of his fights, Bernardo knocked out his opponent and then looked at his wife in the audience and started blowing her kisses with his gloves on and telling her he loved her. The marriage wasn't as picture-perfect as it seemed, though: it ended eight months later. Bernardo's wife ended up taking him for half of everything he was worth, which was a lot of money, since he was a millionaire who drove around in a Ferrari or a Porsche. Athletes in boxing and K-1 make primo money compared to mixed martial artists.

Another tough kickboxer I fought in between my bouts against Mike Bernardo was Jerome Le Banner. Le Banner is an expert in Muay Thai and kickboxing and had been a K-1 superstar since 1995, having faced off in epic battles against Peter Aerts, Ernesto Hoost, Maurice Smith, and Mirko "Cro Cop" Filipovic, to name just a few. Le Banner has been in a lot of wars throughout his long career, and you can see it on his face, with his crooked nose and steely stare. Since he had experience on his side, I used the same strategy I had used against Bernardo and tried to get in his face right away. However, at 6'4", 265 pounds, it would be hard to bum-rush Le Banner, and he was ready for my onslaught.

When Le Banner and I touched gloves in the center of the ring, he slammed his fists down on mine to try and intimidate me. Back in his corner, he was calling me on, opening his eyes really wide and motioning for me to come forward. I glared at him to show him I wasn't scared at all, and I hit myself in the face a bit to try and pump myself up. The huge crowd roared as the two of us tried to psych each other out. Everybody could tell this was going to be great fight — and that it would be over really quickly. Le Banner came at me hard. After hitting me with some punches, he faked a roundhouse kick to the head and hit me with a left low kick that put me off balance. As I was reeling, he came at me, but I covered up well and survived his onslaught. I grabbed the back of Le Banner's head and started nailing him with big right uppercuts until he pushed me off. We exchanged for a bit, but as I went to throw a left jab, he connected with a big overhand right on the chin that knocked me down. I shook my head a bit and got to my feet before the count was done, but my equilibrium wasn't there, and I fell back to the canvas, ending the fight. I had given Le Banner a tough go, but in the end, his experience and size really played to his advantage and he was the better man that night.

Following my fights against Bernardo and Le Banner, I competed in a K-1 super fight against Mark Hunt, a hard hitter from New Zealand. Mark Hunt was a rough customer, having won the World K-1 Grand Prix in 2001. I trained with Maurice Smith and worked a lot on my conditioning for the fight because Hunt had a hard chin, and the myth among K-1 fans was that he couldn't be knocked out. I knew that wasn't true because everybody can be knocked out. But I also knew I would need a good gas tank against him because he was a very patient counter-puncher who carefully picked his spots to explode. I was pretty sure I wouldn't knock him out, so I worked a lot on my technique and my stamina; that way, I could maintain a steady attack throughout the entire fight.

After a quiet first round, we had some good exchanges in the second. I was working the jab a lot and doing a good job of covering up and picking my shots. We exchanged a few really good flurries, but even though we were both throwing bombs, we couldn't knock each other out. At the beginning of final round, Hunt hit me with a hard shot that rocked me. I recovered quickly and told the referee I was all right to keep going. Spitting blood out of my mouth, I stuck out my chin to bait Hunt and then hit him with a big overhand right. He was hurt, so I quickly followed up with a flurry of punches. He managed to recover, but I hit him with some really big combinations at the end of the fight. I felt really good after the fight and had lots of energy left, but the judges gave the unanimous decision win to Hunt.

• • •

My first excursions into K-1 meant I knew exactly what I was getting into when I signed the contract with K-1 after my retirement from

Pride. I had always been a mixed martial artist who preferred the striking aspect of the sport, so when I started fighting in K-1 again, it was a good fit for me. K-1 offered me a fight against Shannon Briggs, a Brooklyn-raised boxer. Briggs had beaten George Foreman for the linear heavyweight title, faced off against Lennox Lewis for the World Boxing Championship heavyweight title, and would later go on to become the World Boxing Organization's Heavyweight Champion.

Shannon Briggs was a rough character with a rough past. I know that he'd been homeless for part of his life and only got into boxing to stay off the streets. For a while, people thought Briggs was going to be the next great American heavyweight. However, in the early '90s, Briggs injured his hand and ended up missing the 1992 Olympic trials. Briggs was best known for beating Foreman, making him the man who beat the man who beat the man, a lineage that traces back from Tyson to Ali and beyond. Briggs didn't hold the title for very long before he was beat by Lennox Lewis, and he's never reached the top again.

One of the reasons K-1 was setting up a fight between me and Briggs was because we had a personal beef. In fact, I hate that guy to this day. It started when he fought Tom Erikson at the K-1 World Grand Prix 2004 in Japan. I was cornering Erikson that night, which was especially significant due to the fact that Briggs and I were scheduled to fight each other several months later.

Briggs, being an experienced boxer, was clearly the heavy favorite going into the fight. Erikson had never competed in kickboxing before, and he's a wrestler, not a striker like Briggs. So, ask yourself, is Briggs, the world champion boxer, going to beat Erikson in his first kick-boxing match? If you could find your asshole with one hand it was easy to figure out who was going to win. Going into the fight, even Erikson knew Briggs outmatched him, but he was trying to stay confident. There was still the chance that Erikson could catch Briggs with a punch and knock him out. Tom had heavy hands and had shown them when he knocked out former UFC heavyweight champion Kevin Randleman with a jab.

At the beginning of their fight, Erikson went out and tried his best, but Briggs did what he needed to do. After setting it up with a left jab, Briggs hit Erikson with a hard right hook that knocked him out. Before the fight, Briggs had seemed really nice, but as soon as he knocked Erikson out, he started acting like he'd built the CN Tower himself. His dreadlocks must have been so tight on his head that he was leaking his brains out or something. It was stupid. Briggs was always going to beat Erikson, and yet, after he won, he started jumping around the ring and jumping on the ropes like he was King Kong.

As I watched Briggs celebrate, I started getting pissed off. That's when Briggs turned, looked at me, and said, "You're next." I guess he was trying to work himself into a frenzy before our scheduled match, but I was furious. Briggs really got my blood boiling, so I got right in his face. I mean, the guy had just knocked out my friend who, at this point, still didn't know who or where he was. I was feeling bad for Erikson lying on the canvas, because I know what he did to make the K-1 show happen. That night, he gave his body to the audience for the show, knowing that he was going to get knocked out. *That* is a true champion. *That* is somebody with a lot of balls. By jumping around the ring and trash-talking a champion fighter like Erikson, Briggs showed no class. He didn't do anything special; he only beat somebody he was supposed to beat.

Even though I was furious, I was happy knowing I was going to be fighting Briggs in a couple of months. I would get my chance to knock him out and pay him back for what he did to my friend. I trained hard on my stand-up and got into top shape for the fight, because I abso-lutely *had* to beat him. There was no way I was going to let Briggs win, so I went out and got the best boxer I could find who could spend time training me in Barrie. The African guy K-1 set me up with was a really good boxer and was almost the same height and weight as Briggs. I paid him $1,000 a week plus his flights and other expenses to come train with me. I put him up in a hotel, and we trained dog-hard at the gym every day, all day long. He was a great help to me, and I was confident that I was going to hand Briggs his ass and give him his first knockout.

Unfortunately, I never did get the chance to repay Briggs for what he did to my friend. At the last minute before our fight, Briggs said he had injured his foot and couldn't compete. Of course, that was complete bullshit. The truth was that Briggs did not want to take a fight with me, because he knew he was going to get beat up. Even though he was being guaranteed $220,000 to fight me, he knew I was going to hand him his ass, and he didn't want that. He's just a big coward. I would fight him on the street if I saw him. I don't care where it is. I hate Shannon Briggs with a passion.

My experience with Briggs proves one of the main differences between boxers and mixed martial artists. Boxers talk so much trash to their opponents, while most mixed martial artists don't. Boxers have to have the mentality that they're going to fight that person to death. To me, that's ghetto shit. This isn't the ghetto; we're professional fighters. Most mixed martial artists know that they've got to go out there and fight their opponent to the best of their ability, and that's the end of the story. In MMA, there's a lot of respect among fighters — very few of them don't get along with each other. For example, Pride sometimes scheduled fights around Christmas, and one Christmas, all of the fighters went to a Korean barbecue for dinner together. There we were at this Korean barbecue, having dinner with people we would be standing toe to toe with a few days later. Mixed martial artists are by far the nicest guys you could imagine. Even after the fights, mixed martial artists usually either congratulate each other or just give a quick nod of encouragement or respect. We realize we're all there for the same reason. I might fight one guy today and another guy tomorrow, but we're all brothers in the same sport. It's a business, so we all know there's no personal animosity.

It's very rare in MMA that people turn things personal in order to fight. I know that Ken Shamrock needed personal vendettas against somebody in order to fight, which is why he hated Tito Ortiz and Don

Frye. In mixed martial arts, Shamrock's an exception; in boxing, those kind of personal vendettas are much more common.

After Briggs decided that he didn't want to get knocked out by me, K-1 set me up against New Zealand's TOA for a super fight at the Battle at Bellagio in Las Vegas. TOA is a ponytailed Samoan who stands 6'4" and weighs 300 pounds. He is a massive man. At the opening bell, TOA came at me hard and fast, backing me into the corner with a big overhand right. However, his punches weren't hurting me, and I showed him that by sticking out my chin. With the crowd cheering me on, I exploded and hit TOA with some hard punches and a hard right low kick that cracked him so hard you could hear it throughout the arena. Once I got him into the corner, I unloaded on him with big combinations and finished with a right hook that knocked him down to the canvas. He stayed down until the very end of the count so I knew he was hurt, but he did manage to get back up. After the restart, I hit him with a combination then stalked him against the ropes, which were the only things keeping him up. After another vicious combination, I finished him off with a big right uppercut that snapped his head back and knocked him down for good. Right away, I looked into the camera and barked, "Where's Shannon Briggs? I want Briggs. Bring Shannon Briggs to me. He's gonna get some of this shit!"

As soon as I left the ring, I went backstage and quickly changed, because Mike Tyson and Muhammad Ali were sitting ringside to present a trophy to the K-1 champion, and I really wanted to go out and meet Ali. As a kid, I grew up watching tapes of his fights, and it was seeing those fights that really inspired me to become a fighter. Ali was an incredible athlete and entertainer, and I just love the guy. In his day, he was a good-looking man with lots of charisma who could always capture the crowds and make people listen.

Even though Muhammad Ali is retired, he is still a big star and needed lots of bodyguards around him so he could enjoy the show without getting mobbed. When I went up to meet Ali, his bodyguards were doing a good job of keeping everybody away, but they immediately recognized me as a fighter whom Ali would want to meet and let me through. Unfortunately, you can't really meet Ali, because he is not really there. You can meet his physical person, but he has so much brain damage that he is not really functioning. Walking up to Ali, I gave him a big hug. As I did that, he leaned into my ear and said one thing to me, "You are one tough nigger." Hearing those words left me momentarily speechless. It was such an incredible honor to be receiving that kind of praise from the greatest boxer of all time. I could only manage to spit out, "Muhammad Ali, I love you man. You are the greatest . . . and we share the same birthday!" Muhammad Ali will always be special, not just because he dominated boxing, but also because he had pizzazz. The aura around him carried him just as far as his boxing skills, and it was a special combination that I've always strived to emulate.

· · ·

Following my disposal of TOA, K-1 invited me to fight at the K-1 World Grand Prix 2004 in Nagoya, Japan. For that fight, they matched me up against Peter "The Dutch Lumberjack" Aerts, a legend in the world of kickboxing. Even though I am older than Aerts, he had way more experience than I did. In 1994, two years before my first fight in the UFC, Aerts competed in the second ever K-1 World Grand Championship, becoming the youngest champion in the history of the organization at the age of 23. A year later, Aerts defended his championship, beating out Ernesto Hoost and Jerome Le Banner along the way. Aerts also won the K-1 World Grand Prix in 1998 and was still one of the top K-1 stars when I fought him.

Since I knew how tough Aerts was going into the fight, I made a big change to my training regimen and had experienced kickboxer Maurice Smith come to my place to train with me for a few months. Smith is an amazing teacher and was able to help retool my style for K-1 by teaching me how to be smart and pick my spots more. He taught me that kickboxing is all about stalking and waiting and, as a result, I became a much more patient fighter. Smith also worked on leg kicks with me — especially avoiding them, since they led to my downfall in my early K-1 fights.

Despite my work on leg kicks, when I stepped into the ring against Aerts for the first time, it was ultimately leg kicks the Dutch Lumberjack used to chop me down. By the end of the first round, I had caught him with a few big shots, but his leg kicks were causing me a lot of pain, and he was dictating the pace of the fight. I was pumped up going into the second round, however, and came out with a ton of shots. The crowd started going nuts as Aerts came back and we both teed off on each other. A right low kick staggered me, and when I bent down, he closed the distance and threw a knee. In the heat of the moment, I forgot we were fighting under K-1 rules, and I picked him up and slammed him down to the mat. Right away, his corner got pissed off and started coming into the ring. Tom Erikson, who was in my corner, was having nothing to do with that, so he yelled at them to get back into their corner, which they quickly did. I got a yellow card for my illegal action and went over to apologize. When the referee restarted, I came out hard and caught Aerts with a few shots that knocked him down. He covered up and then answered back with leg kicks and knees that had me against the ropes until the end of the round.

At the start of the final round, Aerts hit me with a good combination, ending with low kick that dropped me. I could hardly walk, but I got up and told the referee I was good to go. Aerts hit me with another right kick to my left knee, and when I fell down into the ropes, the referee gave me another count. When I stood up to fight again, the crowd cheered at my courage. Aerts knew I was hurt, so he rushed at me and backed me into the corner, hitting me with a bunch of knees, kicks, and punches, before landing another right low kick that sent me falling sideways to the canvas. By that point, I had taken too much punishment and the fight was called.

After the fight, Steve Kalakoda, the guy K-1 had hired to train me, walked up to me and saw my tooth hanging out of my mouth by a couple of gum strings. He ripped the tooth right out of my mouth and said, "Don't worry about it. Let's go, you did good." I didn't know how the tooth had become loose; I just knew that it was sore. Mostly I was concentrating on the pain in my leg: Aerts had torn it up with kicks. It was the worst pain I had ever been in. Aerts is very precise and managed to hit the same part of my leg every time. By the end of the fight, I couldn't even bend my leg — it had swollen up to double its normal size. I had to be helped out of the ring because I couldn't walk. As I was leaving the ring, Aerts came over to congratulate me on a good fight. It had been a war.

Even though I lost to Aerts, I consider my first fight against him as my true entry into K-1. I had already been in some tough fights, but none of them had been as tough as the Aerts fight. That fight really showed K-1 audiences who I was in terms of my heart as a fighter. Aerts is a pioneer in the sport of kickboxing, and his body has gone through more wear and tear than any fighter I have ever known. It was an honor just to compete against somebody else who has the same kind of samurai spirit as me.

During the summer of 2006, just over two years after our first match, I got another chance to fight Peter Aerts, this time at the K-1 World Grand Prix in Sapporo, Japan. Revenge fights had been a popular concept in the early days of K-1, so the company decided to bring back the format, which gave me the chance to avenge my loss. Going into the fight, my plan was to go to the body a lot, forcing Aerts to drop his hands so that I could knock him out. Just as in our first fight, Aerts came out early with some really hard low kicks. After I nailed him with a few overhand rights, he went for a roundhouse kick and I grabbed his leg, hit him with a big shot, and briefly knocked him down. When he got back up, Aerts threw another roundhouse that almost knocked me down. However, I gathered myself and stayed on my feet, covering up against the ropes while he went to town on me until the end of the round.

In round two, Aerts continued with the low kicks as I kept throwing big bombs, trying to knock him out. A left roundhouse staggered me, and I leaned against the ropes covering up until I managed to swing my way out with a few big uppercuts. In the third round, Aerts kept going to the body with legs kicks. I pointed to my gut and told him to hit there again, showing him he wasn't going to finish me with body shots. The rest of the round was busy with both of us going all out. In the end, Aerts won by unanimous decision, but the fight was much closer than the scoreboards indicated.

Both of my fights against Aerts are monumental because they show me coming of age as a fighter. I took a beat-down both times, but I never gave up. In a way, those fights are a kind of trophy saying I still gave my best effort until the last second.

• • •

The year 2005 was a big year for me in K-1. On July 29, I competed in the K-1 World Grand Prix in Hawaii. Over the years, K-1 had outgrown being strictly a Japanese organization and had added 10 tournaments worldwide. Those tournaments decided who would compete in the final K-1 World Grand Prix in Japan. In the first round of the K-1 USA tournament, I fought Wesley "Cabbage" Correira, a hometown guy from Hilo who trained with B.J. Penn. At 6'3", 270 pounds, Cabbage is known as a fighter with a strong chin who can take a lot of punishment. Cabbage is mostly remembered for beating Tank Abbott and for his UFC fights against Andrei Arlovski and Tim Sylvia.

Going into the fight, I was unsure of how I should attack him. I knew that I was going to have to work really hard to beat Cabbage at boxing, because he had a head made of steel and I probably couldn't knock him out. After reviewing some tape, I saw that Cabbage threw a lot of leg kicks in the UFC, so at the last minute, I decided to attack his legs to see if he would be able to receive kicks too.

The fight between us was over quickly. He came out with a flurry of punches and tried pushing me against the ropes. After I covered up, I pushed Cabbage off me and then attacked him with leg kicks and some big left hooks that rocked him. From the minute I landed the first leg kick, he started wincing. As soon as I saw pain, I knew I had the right game plan. I was playing a little rope-a-dope, letting Cabbage hit me and calling him on, Ali-style. I got off the ropes with some big punches and then chased him around the ring with some right and left hooks that were landing flush and had him reeling. I could tell Cabbage was hurt, so I kept the pressure on and finally, with 45 seconds left in the first round, I hit him with a hard kick right behind the knee that crippled him. Immediately, the referee stepped in and sent us to our corners. Cabbage tried to shake it off but was clearly in a lot of pain. As soon as the fight restarted, I chased him around the ring and landed another low kick that sent him down again. This time, the fight was called off: Cabbage couldn't continue due to the pain in his leg.

After quickly disposing of Cabbage, I fought Carter "The Beast" Williams in the K-1 Grand Prix semi-finals. Carter Williams is a big, stocky guy with thick legs who trained in Muay Thai with Team Voodoo USA in California. I didn't think much of him as a fighter. As in the Cabbage fight, it didn't take me long to dispose of Williams. I had a bit of a size advantage over him, and as soon as I unloaded with some big right hooks, he crumpled to the canvas. Williams got up at the last second of the count, but once the fight started again, I quickly bum-rushed him. After a big combination knocked him silly, he dropped for good, giving me a first-round knockout.

In the finals of the K-1 USA tournament, I fought Yusuke Fujimoto, who trained with Monster Factory in Japan. Fujimoto was a Japan Grand Prix finalist, but I was favored going into the fight. I felt much more powerful than Fujimoto, and I knew that he would have to fight like a dog in order to beat me. Up until that point, I had had some easy matches and I was fresh and ready to go. I was feeling good and tried to run right through him. I knew he was tired, so I just kept pushing the pace.

Fujimoto started out by throwing a lot of leg kicks, so I opened up with some big hooks that dropped him. He got up and came at me right away, ducking and throwing punches. Countering, I landed a left hook right on the chin that sent him into the ropes and to the canvas. Fujimoto barely made it out for the start of the second round and kept covering up and ducking. He tried a couple of roundhouse kicks that looked fancy but weren't doing anything. With less than one minute left in the second round, I scored another knockdown with some perfectly placed big right overhands and some hooks. I could tell Fujimoto was tired, because his defenses started to come down and he was just trying to make it out of the round. At the end of the second round, I hugged him and was smiling and bouncing around, because I knew that I had him beat.

I came out hard at the beginning of the third, hitting Fujimoto with a big straight right and some leg kicks. After a big roundhouse kick and some hard hooks, he hit the canvas but still managed to get back up, much to the crowd's delight. Once we restarted, a couple of low kicks sent him down in pain. By that point, Fujimoto's corner had seen enough damage and threw in the towel at 1:19 of the third round. Fujimoto was down for a long time in obvious pain and I took the time to celebrate. After Bruce Buffer announced me as the new K-1 World Grand Prix USA Champion, I was handed a large trophy and went over to hug and shake hands with Fujimoto. It felt great to be the champ again; it was the first time I had won a championship since the International Vale Tudo Championship in Brazil. It was that win that secured me a berth in the K-1 World Grand Prix in Osaka, Japan, and a second fight against Jerome Le Banner.

• • •

Less than a year after winning that fight, I competed in another K-1 World Grand Prix at the Mirage Hotel in Las Vegas. Going into it, I was one of the favorites to win the whole thing. In the first round of the tournament, I fought Kengo Watanabe, a former Japanese rugby star who had switched to mixed martial arts. Starting out with the Pancrase organization in Japan, Kengo had faced some tough competition, including Bas Rutten, Ron Waterman, and Lyoto Machida. Our match in Las Vegas was Kengo's first foray into kickboxing, and after I was done with him, it would be his last.

From the opening bell, Kengo came out and tried to get into a brawl with me. It was a bad idea. I unleashed a combination of hard punches, ending with a big right hand that landed directly on Kengo's temple, knocking him out only 40 seconds into the fight. As soon as the punch landed, Kengo folded over and fell forward unconscious onto the ground. Kengo's eyes were wide open, but he was completely out of it. He couldn't even stand for a while, and when the ringside officials tried to get him up, he quickly had to lie back down.

In my second match of the evening, I faced Scott Lighty, a guy I had fought once before in 2005. Scott Lighty came out of "The Pit," the same tough training camp run by John Hackleman that had produced Chuck Liddell. In our first fight, I learned that Lighty is a chicken — he runs from anything you throw at him. He's a great kid, but he gets intimidated too easily, and I quickly downed him with leg kicks. Going into our rematch and our semi-final fight, I figured I was still in his head from the last time. As soon as the bell rang, I brought the heat to Lighty and knocked him down just seven seconds into the fight. Lighty took an eight count and got back up, but when the fight restarted, I hit him with a left and a glancing right hook that knocked him down again. Lighty got up and wanted to keep fighting, but the referee saw that he wasn't really with it and ended the fight. The win over Lighty earned me a berth in the finals of the K-1 World Grand Prix USA for the second time in less than a year.

In the finals, I was matched against Chalid "The Fist" Arrab. Chalid, a Moroccan-German, entered the tournament as a heavy underdog. Most of his wins were by knockout, which meant he had heavy hands. Earlier in the night, Chalid had knocked out wrestler Sean O'Haire in the first round. In the semi-finals, Chalid actually lost to Carter Williams. But Williams didn't want to fight a fresh Gary Goodridge, so he backed out of the fight. Chalid, who was already in the ambulance on his way to the hospital, took some stitches and came back for the opportunity to face me in the finals. Now *that* is an example of a warrior!

Early in the first round, I landed a big left hook that sent Chalid face-first into the canvas. When he got back up, he attacked me, but he wasn't inflicting any damage. I was covering up and just waiting for him to stop before I was going to explode. In the second round, I scored another early knockdown. Chalid hit the ground but quickly stood up, and we went at it again before the referee could step in. When we finally clinched, the referee pulled us apart and awarded me the knockdown. The rest of the round was pretty even — we just stood in front of each other and brawled.

Going into the third and final round, I knew I was ahead on all of the judges' scorecards, but I didn't just want to win a decision. I can't stop myself from going for the knockout. At that point, other fighters might have gone into defensive mode to protect the win, but that's just not me. I give Chalid a lot of credit. One of us was hitting the floor, and it just happened to be me. I had a big right hand coming his way, but his right hook got to my jaw first and knocked me out. I don't know what the hell happened, because I never should've lost to Chalid. I didn't even see a punch coming; I just woke up on the floor. Since I had won the first two rounds, if I had gotten up, I would've won the fight. However, Chalid had nailed me good and I didn't know where I was. After the fight, Chalid and I both ended up in the hospital together. It was pretty funny: after beating each other up, we were practically bedmates.

CHAPTER **TWELVE**

Toward the end of my career, I took a lot of fights against tough up-and-comers in the fight game. Keeping active allowed me to compete in the odd, big show against world-class competition. On August 5, 2007, I fought Hong-Man Choi, a 7'2", 350-pound giant of a man from South Korea. The reason Choi is so big is because he has pituitary gigantism, a disease that means he can't stop growing. Due to his huge size advantage, Choi was extremely dangerous against anybody and had beaten the likes of Bob Sapp and Semmy Schilt. I didn't have a strategy going into the fight because it was impossible for me come up with proper training partners who were 7'2". The tallest training partner I had was Jan Nortje, and at 6'9" he was *still* short compared to Choi.

In the fight, I tried to land some big overhand rights, but Hong-Man Choi was able to use kicks to effectively keep his distance. Choi was just so bloody big. When I tried to close the distance to where I could land strikes, I would catch knees. However, if I stayed on the outside, I'd get hit with hard jabs. I had to think of a plan immediately but I couldn't come up with one quick enough: Choi nailed me with a big knee that sent me down to the canvas. I wasn't knocked out, but I might as well have been because I don't remember any of it. I had started out my career as the Goliath in a David and Goliath match. With Choi, I got the opportunity to find out what it was like to be the David.

In the summer of 2008, I got a last-minute call to face Paul Buentello at Affliction: Banned in Anaheim, California. Affliction was being co-promoted by the Affliction Clothing Company and Adrenaline MMA, with financial backing from some big celebrities like Donald Trump and Mark Cuban. Over the past few years I had fought in lots of countries like Hungary, Lithuania, Korea, China, Latvia, Czech Republic, the Netherlands, and Romania, and it was nice to be able to fight on North American soil again. Buentello was originally slated to face Fedor Emelianenko's brother, Aleksander, but "Aleks" couldn't get cleared to fight, so Affliction hired me to do the job. Originally, I was going to California just to watch the event. I had no idea I was going to fight until my plane landed, and my manager told me I had been offered the fight, which began in 22 minutes. There aren't many other fighters out there who would take a fight with such little notice. Not only did I have less than a half hour to prepare, I also had no corner men, no shorts, and no mouth guard. Worst of all, neither Tom Erikson or my sister Susie were there with me.

Going into the fight, most people thought Buentello was going to knock me out in the first round because he hits hard as hell. Since Buentello was in my weight class, I had always looked at his fights and thought I'd be a good matchup against him. I thought Buentello didn't have enough to beat me, so I jumped at the opportunity to fight him right away. In the end, I was quite surprised by Buentello. I planned to drop some kicks on his legs to soften him up, causing him to lower his hands so that I could knock him out. However, he kept hitting me with hard left jabs throughout the entire fight. His left jabs were so hard they felt like straight rights when he hit me. Buentello certainly doesn't look like a hard puncher, but in reality, the guy hits bloody hard — his punching technique is just perfect. Buentello couldn't knock me out the way many people had predicted. Instead, he only squeaked by with a decision win. Not bad for a 42-year-old against a fighter many people considered a top 10 heavyweight at the time.

Lately, it's been a lot harder for me to train for fights because of the wear and tear on my body. One really painful injury I'm dealing with is a bad sciatic nerve. I've gone for physiotherapy and chiropractic work, but they haven't been able to help me. Painkillers don't work for me either. On a normal day, I have to sit down at least once every hour because there is pain shooting up my whole leg and my toes are numb. Oftentimes if I'm going out somewhere, I'll be in incredible pain by the time I reach my car. I can't wait in line at stores. I can't even walk down to the park with my kids.

In 2008, I fought Terroll Dees from the U.S. at the Iroquois MMA Championships in Ontario, Canada. It was a fight I was really excited about accepting, because it was close enough to my hometown that all of my friends and family could attend. Unfortunately, two months before the fight I couldn't even stand for two minutes, let alone run on the treadmill. I could only do a little bit of training before I'd have to sit down. In the end, I lost a three-round decision to Dees, but it really doesn't matter. I could've won; he had nothing. For a 26-year-old, Dees looked old and fought old. I know that he trained hard because it was a big chance for him to fight me. Still, Dees didn't even once make me dizzy or make me think about holding up my hands. I'd fight him again at any event and I'd even fight him for free. Don't pay me any-thing; pay Dees all of the money. It's not about revenge — I just want to let him know he didn't do anything. I'd bum-rush him and the fight would be done in two minutes.

Along with having a bad sciatic nerve, I have also had to have sur-geries on my gums and teeth. The problem first started when I fought Fedor and he had me down on the ground, caving my face in. One of Fedor's punches severely loosened my front left tooth and, after that, it was always loose and it never got set properly. I thought that if I left the tooth alone, it would eventually heal on its own. But it never did. I also screwed up another tooth in a fight against Glaube "The Brazilian Warrior" Feitosa. Feitosa and I fought each other twice, but it was in the second fight that he really injured me. In our first fight, at K-1 World Grand Prix 2005 in Las Vegas, Feitosa knocked me out with a left high kick in the first round. Even though Feitosa had a quick KO win over me, I knew that I stood a chance to knock him out if we fought again. He had great kicks and was really tough, but I felt that I could attack the body and get him to drop his hands for long enough to end the fight with big uppercut or hook.

Going into my rematch against Feitosa at the K-1 World Grand Prix 2005 in Japan, I really wanted to win because beating him was going to be a big feather in my cap. Throughout the fight, Feitosa was kicking my ass from corner to corner with kicks. However, I have a problem in that I'm stupid and will never give up. I've always got a puncher's chance as long as I just stay awake and alive. In the second round, Feitosa was kicking the shit out of me and pushed one of my front teeth right out of my mouth right with a front kick. During a break in the action, I pointed at my tooth on the ground and the referee picked it up. On the video of the fight you can see the huge gap where the tooth used to be. Even though my mouth was filled with blood, I was all right; the referee just shoved my mouth guard back in and restarted the fight. In between the second and third rounds, my corner worked feverishly to try to clear all of the blood off my face and out of my nose. The third round was pretty even and I had a big flurry of strikes at the end, but it wasn't enough: Feitosa ended up winning by unanimous decision. He was the better man in both fights.

After my first tooth was knocked out, I had to get it replaced, which took about a year to get going. As soon as I was ready for the final surgery, Feitosa knocked out another tooth, forcing me to wait another year. Only recently have I gotten around to finishing the process. What happens when you get your teeth knocked out is that it rips the bone, the gum, the flesh, and everything else right out of your mouth. It's not like you've simply lost a tooth. You can even see the bone through the ripped gums. When I went in for surgery, the doctor had to take cow bone, mix it with human bone, and pack it in there so that it would grow. In order to do it, they had to cut my gum and then scrape the bone. I was awake during the surgery, and with the doctor scraping at my gums to get to the bone. I couldn't feel any pain, but I could feel a lot of pressure. After packing in new bone, the doctor had to put in cadaver gum because I didn't have any extra gum. It sounds like a horrible experience, but that doctor did the best job he'd ever done, and I really appreciate all of the work that he did on me.

The whole procedure ended up costing just over $20,000. Thankfully, it was entirely covered by K-1. I didn't want to wait until the end of my career to get my injuries fixed, like some fighters do. I wanted to get my teeth fixed while I was still under contract with K-1. During my time with the UFC and Pride, I never had any really severe injuries. In contrast, fighting in K-1 messed me up. The sport of mixed martial arts is the easiest thing I have ever done, a walk in the park. On the other hand, K-1 is a very dangerous sport. The trauma that goes along with training in kickboxing on a day-to-day basis is the toughest thing I've ever done.

• • •

For a brief time in 2009, I had a gym in Barrie called Fight University. A couple of friends had asked me what I thought about opening up a mixed martial arts gym. At first, I wasn't sure if I wanted to do it. I didn't mind opening a gym, but I didn't want to put up all of the money. I've been a part of many business ventures before, and every time I have put up all of the money and the business ended up falling apart. I went into the pick and pack business with a friend of mine and ended up losing tens of thousands of dollars. I didn't know anything about the business; I was just the financier behind it and ended up losing my shirt. When I decided to open Fight University, I tried to make things a little safer for myself, so that I was not the one left holding the bucket if the whole thing failed. Though ultimately the business failed, it was a venture much closer to me than picking and packing.

Fight University was supposed to teach people every aspect of MMA. When new students came in, we'd work on whatever they needed to work on, even if it was just getting in shape. Fight University offered everything from fighting techniques to nutritional information. If the students were completely new to combat sports, we'd start with some balance drills so they would know the basics. If they had more advanced skills, we'd help them get to the point where they were ready to step into the cage and put it all on the line. I used to tell all of the up-and-coming fighters in the gym that you have to have an open mind and always be willing to try new things. There's nothing wrong with trying and failing. Everybody out there has tried and failed. A champion is someone who continues trying until they are successful.

Along with opportunities like being able to open a training facility, being a fighter also gave me the opportunity to help others who are fighting for something. I've always loved trying to help children. I've won over a thousand arm-wrestling trophies, and I used to love giving away the trophies to less-fortunate children or to homes for children with special needs. Every summer I'd volunteered on fishing and hunting trips with terminally ill children in California. Tom Erikson, Don Frye, Bill Goldberg, and some famous hockey players also go every year. When we go down there, we have a blast. It's all about the children, but it's also a chance for us friends to get together. We make sure we have a good time, because if we're having a good time, then the kids are going to have a good time. Every time I go there, I'm excited to get up in the morning and sorry to go to bed at night. The first year I went, I knew that all of the children were sick, but I didn't know that they were terminally ill. I later found out that out of 10 kids on the excursion, only three of them had survived the year. I felt terrible when I heard that, but all of us were glad to have been able to give those kids a little bit of happiness and the chance to meet some sports figures before they died.

Being a fighter has given me the chance to take part in some pretty crazy ventures. Recently, Art Davie, the same promoter who gave me my first fight in the UFC, invited me to compete in a new sport that he helped create called XARM, or Extreme Arm-wrestling. The concept behind XARM was some weird shit; it was a mix of arm-wrestling and mixed martial arts. Two contestants were tethered to a table and then, during three one-minute rounds, they would have to try and pin each other's arm while striking or choking them. Basically, you're arm-wrestling while beating the shit out of your opponent in a knockdown drag-out kind of fight. The concept was exciting, because you didn't know what was going to happen. There were obvious problems with the sport though. For one, it was easier to knock someone out then to pin them, but pinning your opponent was what got you the most points. As a result, the guy who ends up winning would be going for the pins over fighting. Another problem was that there were no safety precautions in place. There was no testing for anything and people could potentially get cut and exchange bodily fluids. At first, XARM seemed like a good thing for me to take part in, but they weren't offering me any money, and I didn't want to be taking punches for no reason.

In late 2009, I got a call to fight Gegard Mousasi at Dynamite!! 2009 in Saitama, Japan. At 24 years old, Mousasi entered our match on a 14-fight winning streak, a run that included winning the 2008 DREAM Middleweight Grand Prix. After that, he moved up to light heavyweight division and defeated Renato "Babalu" Sobral for the Strikeforce light-heavyweight title. I took the fight against Mousasi on less than one week's notice. I knew that FEG, the promotor behind K-1 and DREAM, was in need of a fighter and I really needed the $30,000 I was being offered. I had a lot of bills that need paying around that time, so it seemed like a real blessing. The fight didn't last very long, as Mousasi took me down and beat me in the first round by TKO.

After the fight, FEG decided they didn't want to pay me. It took over a year for me to see a single penny of the money I was owed for that fight. It really pissed me off because I spent my entire career fighting for them and I had never experienced this problem with them before. FEG stopped returning my phone calls and ignored me altogether. They didn't tell me what was going on at all. I wanted to give them the benefit of the doubt, but when it became clear that I wasn't getting paid, I turned to my fans and the media to help put some pressure on the Japanese company. I traveled all the way to Japan on short notice and sacrificed my body for them and yet FEG still tried to screw me. It pisses me off, because I'm worth more than that. I know FEG is having financial difficulties, but that's no excuse, especially since they continue to put on shows. They really need to look at changing their payment schedule, because guys like me can't afford to not get paid in a timely fashion.

During another recent fight against Nemeth "Tatar" Gabor in Budapest, Hungary, not only did I have to fight him, I also had to fight the referee. When the first round started, I hit Gabor with some pretty hard leg kicks, and when he counter-attacked, I covered up, knowing he was going to tire out. While I was covering up, the referee stopped the match and took a point away from me. I couldn't believe it. My corner was protesting the point deduction, but it didn't make much of a difference and the match continued. I started attacking Gabor's legs again and was really starting to inflict some damage. However, whenever we were against the ropes, Gabor would hold onto the ropes with his armpits. And it wasn't just a couple of times that he did this; he ended up doing it a few dozen times to keep himself up. Since the referee wasn't doing anything to discourage Gabor from continuing to use the ropes, I decided to take matters into my own hands by getting behind Gabor and grabbing his legs to pull him off the ropes. At that point, the referee stopped the match, but when he restarted, he still hadn't taken any points away from Gabor. I wanted to be sure that he couldn't use the ropes so I took him right down to the mat. While I was on top of him and looking for an arm bar, all of a sudden and for no apparent reason, the referee stopped the fight again and made us stand up.

I started to really hurt Gabor with some knees in the second round, but every time, he would grab onto the ropes. I looked to the referee to intervene, but he wouldn't do anything. It got to the point where my corner man, John Gnap, would slap Gabor's hands to try and keep him from holding onto the ropes. Finally, I'd had enough of that game, so when the referee tried to start us up again, I just walked out of the ring. The whole scenario seemed like a joke: there was no effort on behalf of the referee or Gabor to fight by the rules we had agreed upon. It was the first time I walked out of the ring in my entire career. There was no way I could participate in that anymore so I just got out of my fight gear, showered, and left the venue. It was an unfortunate ending, but I needed to stand up for myself. Sometimes the fight is not just between you and your opponent; the third man in the ring is the referee, and he can have the biggest impact on the fight.

The Gabor fight brings up a lot of the problems associated with fighting in a foreign country. When you're behind enemy lines, it's pretty intimidating; you don't know what might happen. There are times when you start to think to yourself, *Man, if I knock this mother-fucker out, I'm gonna have to fight my way outta here!* You honestly think the crowd could turn on you if things go badly. That's what happened when I fought Tadas Rinkevicius at K-1 Hero's in Lithuania. I went in there and I floored their hometown boy. While he was down on the ground trying to pick his lips up, I danced over top of him wanting to smack him down some more. I thought for sure I was going to have to fight the crowd. There are times when people want to spit on you on your way out of the arena, because their boy just got his ass kicked. You just have to deal with it; you can't fight back the entire crowd. It's not like professional wrestling, where if your favorite guy gets knocked down, he gets up and fights some more. That shit ain't real; this stuff is the real deal. Watching it on television, you don't normally get to see it, but, especially in the smaller local shows, people get right into the fights.

North America isn't immune to the type of problems I've faced with promotions overseas, which is why commissions need to start increasing their regulations. At Major Fight League 3 in Montreal, Quebec, I agreed to fight a guy named Tom Murphy. The fight was at a heavyweight level, which was no big deal based on the fact that I was walking around at about 250 pounds. Then, just a few weeks before the fight, the promoter, Dirk Waardenburg, told me I had to get down to 215 in order to participate. It didn't make any sense at all. I guess the commission decided to make up some sort of catchweight bout of whatever weight they wanted. I told them I wasn't going below 240 pounds, but they agreed to 220. I'd never had to cut weight before in my entire career, but I agreed to the terms and dieted and trained my ass off. I was in some of the best shape of my life, but I knew the whole situation with the promotion wasn't right from the start.

A few weeks before the fight, I spoke to Dirk on the phone, and he promised to pay me $5,000 that the commission was to be told about, and an extra $5,000 in cash they were not going to know about. Half of it prior to the bout, and half after. In the days leading up to the fight, and right up until I was supposed to walk out and fight, Dirk made excuses as to why he couldn't pay me the full amount right away. When my corner man and I confronted him, he kept saying that he couldn't pay me because there were too many people around. That didn't make any sense — there were lots of places we could go to exchange money. I told Dirk I wasn't going out there to fight unless he paid me. He offered to give me a little bit of money and told me he just couldn't afford to pay me the rest. I handed the money back to him and I told him I wasn't going to fight. After what happened to me in Japan with FEG's non-payment, I didn't want to risk it. Even if I was totally convinced I was going to win, it's a matter of principle. There was no way I was going to go out there like an idiot and do my job but not get paid for it. It was a tough decision. I could've used that little bit of money he had given me to help pay for some bills.

CHAPTER **THIRTEEN**

Taking punches is something I just don't want to be doing anymore. I'm at a place right now where I never really want to fight again. I'm in my mid-40s, and the game has changed a whole lot since I started. I'm not at the level I should be at to compete, so I have no interest and no motivation to keep training. For me to get back into the ring and fight someone who's half my age for $20,000 is just not worth it anymore. I don't need to be an organic punching bag for anyone. It's just not in me, and I can't train for it anymore, so I'm looking for another job to make some money and support my children.

There comes a time in everybody's life when you have to make a decision on what path to take. Right now I have to take a path other than professional fighting. I'm a competitor and I want to win. If I can't win anymore, it's time for me to move on. When all is said and done, I wanted to be remembered as a no-nonsense kind of guy who took no prisoners. I wasn't fighting for decisions or submissions; I always fought to knock somebody out and give the crowd an exciting fight. I can only hope that the fans recognize and appreciate that. As I've gotten older, things have relaxed and I've mellowed out a little bit, but I will always have a fighter's heart and a samurai spirit.

If I could do anything, I would like to be a gynecologist simply because there are a lot of openings in that job. All kidding aside, I'd like to divorce my wife so that I can set her free. Then I'd like to get re-married, raise my kids, and find a job. I can do anything and live happily ever after because I've done it all. I see myself as a blue-collar worker who went into a sport, became a full-time athlete, and then became a blue-collar worker again. I've won the game of life already. I came from virtually nothing and ended up on top of the world.

People want to know why I would fight when I could have done any other job out there. Why did I fight? What drives somebody to be a fighter? Why do you want to make a living punching people in the face? When people ask me those sorts of questions, I always say that everything is a means to an end. I mean, why would somebody want to go to school for eight years to be doctor or a lawyer? I tell them we all have our little niches in this world. We all have things we're good at, and fighting just happens to be what I was good at. I'm a fighter. Why do I want to fight? There are several different reasons. When I first started out, it was fame and notoriety. I wanted to win UFC 8 and be a champion of something. I was already the world arm-wrestling champion and I thought I could be a champion fighter as well. On top of that, I knew I stood to win $50,000. Beyond that, it never really crossed my mind that I would do it again. I just thought about winning that one UFC. However, I quickly realized that even though I didn't win the $50,000, I could still make money at this sport and that idea began to play with my head.

Fighting was fairly easy money, but it was easy money for being punched in the face. That's not to mention getting kicked or getting a broken bone. Those things sound pretty rough for the average person, but for a fighter, it's nothing, just part of the game. You might break something, but you fight through it. Sure it hurts, but you're going to get over it. You might break your jaw because you got punched in the mouth or kicked in the mouth, but you get over it. I lost two teeth from fighting, and it isn't a big deal. The only reason it bothers me is because I'm very vain about what I look like. But, like I said, it's all just part of the game. My job is to finish the person in front of me in order to be asked to come back and make more money. Also, who doesn't want to be the best at their job? When you're a pilot, you want to be the best pilot. You want to be able to land that plane smoothly. It's the same with me. If my job was to beat somebody up, I wanted to beat them up good. I wanted people to look back and say, "Wow, Gary Goodridge got paid to fight and he came in and did his job!"

When I first started fighting, everything was about winning. At that point, I really didn't care about how much money I was making. However, as the years went on, I started to think more about money than winning. You get trapped by everything that starts to catch up with you. By everything, I'm talking about bills, taxes, child support — just the lifestyle in general. It starts off pretty slow, but it sure does pick up at a pretty good pace. After that point, it's all about cash. So right now it's not about winning, it's about cash. I think that anybody who's gone through the type of career that I've gone through will tell you the same thing. Lately, I've just been broke. I'm looking for a job all the time. I need money to pay my bills.

The worst injuries in fighting are the ones you can't really see right away. The head injuries that accumulate over the years. Concussions aren't like cuts that you can stitch up. Even when I would take some major hits, I would never complain about a headache, and there were never really any immediate symptoms of damage. I always went to see a doctor when I was fighting in Pride and K-1. Both of the organizations took really good care of me in terms of checking me out. I had to have an MRI before every fight, and because I was fighting so often, my head was looked at quite often. If there was something insidious there, they probably would've picked up on it between one of the fights.

The effects of brain damage on my life have really become noticeable in the last two or three years. At first, a lot of people thought I was joking when I started forgetting things. I was always joking around, so people thought that I was just playing a game. It became clear after a while that I wasn't just playing a game. Sometimes I can tell that my speech is really impaired, compared to what it used to be. At times, it's hard to dig out a noun when I'm trying to express something. Things just aren't processing the same way that they did before. It certainly doesn't happen all the time, but sometimes my close friends and family will have to bring me back to what I was talking about. I'll call them for something and then completely forget what it was I was calling about. I've always been intelligent and have had a great sense of humor, but I definitely notice that I'm not as quick-witted anymore. I used to love talking on the phone and would have conversations that lasted for eight hours, talking about all kinds of incredible things. It's harder now to keep focused on a conversation for more than a couple of minutes.

My short-term memory loss has gotten progressively worse over the last few years. It's particularly bad when I'm under a lot of stress, which can be scary, because I've been dealing with more and more stress in the last little while. It's scary because it's something that's really becoming a big problem in combat sports. It's not just fighters — we're seeing the effects of brain damage with football players, hockey players, and even soccer players. It's a problem in any sport that involves traumatic head stress.

Short-term memory loss is not the only a problem I'm dealing with now. If you ask some people who have known me for their entire lives, there's been a personality change as well. It's a scary thing for me to have to deal with, especially because of the history of mental illness in my family. It's not easy to admit, but people close to me have said that I'm a shadow of the Gary Goodridge I used to be. I mean, I was never a rocket scientist or anything, but I was always very witty. It might surprise people to know I was a very good singer in my arm-wrestling heydays. Phil and I would go to arm-wrestling tournaments together, and I would try and entertain him the whole time, just singing away. I knew the words to so many songs from start to finish. I used to do great versions of "Baby Got Back" by Sir Mix-A-Lot and Michael Jackson's "Thriller." Now my ability to recall lyrics is lessened, and my sense of melody is not the same as it once was.

I've tried to help people out, but unfortunately that means getting taken advantage of sometimes. It sucks, but I've been ripped off by so many guys who have come in and out of my life just trying to make a quick buck. I used to have a lot of money, but I'm struggling now. When I became a star in the UFC, I made a choice: I decided to be done with my job at Honda so I could pursue my fighting career. One of the consequences is that I've got no benefits and no pension. I would have those things if I'd stayed at Honda, but I made the choice to keep fighting.

Some of my close friends won't even discuss fighting with me. I guess they don't want me to think that it's okay to keep doing it. They saw the threat that fighting posed and the damage it was doing and don't want to see me get another concussion. They don't want me to have an aneurysm or a stroke. Some of my friends think that the brain damage started to become most noticeable after some of my K-1 fights. Lately, the people who are closest to me tell me I should go to the doctor and get some tests done to prove that I've got brain damage. Perhaps that way I can get a disability check. There are not many jobs that I'm really capable of doing — my back is also in such bad shape that I can barely stand up — and I'm afraid that I might someday lose my house.

When it comes to fighting, it's pretty obvious that the fire that used to be in my eyes is gone. Back in the day, I had no fear in my eyes. If I ever got beat, I would go back to the drawing board and figure out how to win. I've been beaten up so badly for so long that I now don't have the confidence or the pride I used to. The truth is, I'm just doing it for the money, and I'll compete even though I know I'm going to lose. When I had the fire in my eyes, I never would have put myself in that position, but, over the last several years, I've lost most of my confidence. I'm fighting for one thing and one thing only: the money.

There has been a lot of discussion in the Canadian medical community about the regulation of mixed martial arts. I hope the people making the decisions realize the widespread popularity of the sport and the importance of regulation. By legalizing the sport, the government would be able to ensure there is strict medical licensing, insurance, and other safeguards in place. While there's been some work done connecting boxing to mental illness later on in life, there is very little relevant information about the brain damage in mixed martial arts because it is such a new sport. A lot of people think that MMA is safer than boxing because there are fewer head shots. This type of talk takes the focus away from the fact that there are still long-term consequences for mixed martial artists who suffer multiple concussions. I'm worried that the mood changes and the symptoms of mental illness are only going to increase over the next few years of my life. I worry about how I'm going to be able to pay for my own medical expenses, let alone take care of my daughters.

It is kind of ironic that when I first watched the UFC I thought it was barbaric. I didn't think there was any way I could do it, but I had a lot of bravado and my curiosity was piqued. A lot of people might see me as just a fighter, but I've had several other careers and I've always been interested in helping people outside of the fight game. I've never been a typical meathead; instead, I always prided myself on being caring, well educated, and goal-oriented. I've devoted a lot of time to the future of my children and I've tried to be a positive role model and teach them that their strength comes from within.

I hope that my fans can learn from the incredible experiences I've had throughout my life. I came from absolute poverty, and yet, here I am: a former star athlete who has written an autobiography. My mother was the matriarch of the Goodridge family and she is responsible for the success that my sisters and I have had. She always taught us that if we can dream it and believe it, we will be able to achieve it. The life of a fighter is definitely not for everybody. I've taken my lumps and my bumps, and I hope I've given you an honest picture about what it's like to fight for your entire life. Thanks to my family, my friends, and everyone else who has ever loved me or helped me along the way . . . happy humping.

ACKNOWLEDGMENTS

Barbra Goodridge, my sisters Sharon, Shirma, Susie and Lisa, Mike Mobbs, Phil Stoppert, Michael Hunter, Phong Tran, John Gnap, Norm Bell, Andrew McMichael, Tom Erikson, Karen Goodridge, Mike Garrow, and Michael Holmes. And to our family and friends and the many Big Daddy fans who helped inspire and encourage this project.